Steps on the Way

The Journey of The Scottish Episcopal Church

1513-2013

Gerald Stranraer-Mull

The money from the sale of this book is for

"For the Right Reasons"

a charity working in Merkinch, an area of Inverness which is one of the most deprived in Scotland. More than forty percent of the working age population is unemployed and ten per cent of all those living there receive incapacity benefit or disability living allowance.

"For the Right Reasons" is there to help those who wish to overcome drug or alcohol dependency. It gives unconditional, un-judgemental support and friendship throughout the process.

© Gerald Stranraer-Mull 2013

Printed and published in 2013 by
"For the Right Reasons"
60 Grant Street
Inverness IV3 8BS
Telephone 01463 718844 and 07717457247

ISBN 978-1-905787-81-4

This book is dedicated to the memory of Albert Reed, an inspiring teacher of history at Woodhouse Grove School

and to

The people of the Diocese of Aberdeen and Orkney, at whose 2012 Conference this book had its beginning. And to everyone past and present, at Saint Mary-on-the-Rock at Ellon and Saint James at Cruden Bay who shared the journey with me. I am ever grateful.

Contents

A First Word	Page 5
Chapter 1 – The Beginning	Page 6
Chapter 2 – Episcopalian – the enduring appeal	Page 11
Chapter 3 – A background to Reformation and Revolution	Page 13
Chapter 4 – The 16th century	
Flodden	Page 18
The Chronological Story	Page 24
Castle of Martyrdom and Murder	Page 31
Chapter 5 – The 17th century	
The Honours of Scotland	Page 35
The Chronological Story	Page 37
Glasgow Cathedral's Reformation	Page 52
Chapter 6 – The 18th century	
Priests of Culloden	Page 54
The Chronological Story	Page 58
True love ends in tears	Page 71
Chapter 7 – The 19th century	
Persecution and An Argument are over	Page 74
The Chronological Story	Page 79
A faithful priest	Page 94
Chapter 8 -- The 20th century	
Two country churches – their story	Page 98
The Chronological Story	Page 103
Nuns come to Shetland	Page 122
Chapter 9 – The 21st century	Page 127
Chapter 10 – What's Ahead	Page 134
Further Reading	Page 135

A First Word

*At each midnight another day slips into history.
But, when we listen with the ear of the heart,
it is possible to hear the echo of ones gone by.*

Welcome to these pages which tell the story of the Scottish Episcopal Church. It is a story of people. Apart from the opening chapters and the vignettes of "A Moment in the Century", which begin and end each of the chapters covering the 16th to 20th centuries, it is presented as a chronological series of dates.

Behind all the dates there are real people – good, bad, indifferent – seeking to find and express the truth of God. None succeeded perfectly, but they tried. Whether their lives were peaceful or turbulent, all will have known the same hopes and fears that we do.

And that is what makes history fascinating. It has a pattern and emotion because it is about people. We are affected by it, as history is not just the past - it influences the present and shapes the future too.

**Gerald Stranraer-Mull
Muir of Ord
July 2013**

Chapter 1
The Beginning

The story of the Scottish Episcopal Church is traced here but it cannot be entirely separated from the story of the other Churches in Scotland or those elsewhere in the United Kingdom and beyond.

The Episcopal Church's story traditionally begins with the Reformation in 1560, but our chronological account goes back further and starts at the Battle of Flodden five hundred years ago this year. James IV, a deeply pious and yet flawed King of Scots, died in the battle as did many of the leaders of both Church and Nation. The vacuum it created led to heightened expectations of the emerging Reformation and also harsh measures to seek to repress it.

The King's death at Flodden is the first of *"What might have happened if....."* situations which have occurred throughout the history of the Church (the detailed examination of which is not part of this book). Other such questions include..... *What might have happened had James VII been more accommodating?.....What if the Scottish bishops had accepted the regime of William and Mary?.....What if Bonnie Prince Charlie had pressed on from Derby?......What if he had fought a guerrilla war in the mountains rather than the Battle of Culloden?*

But, to begin at the beginning, we need to go back further still....... From the time of the earliest Christians in our land, who were probably soldiers in the Roman Legions, until 1560 there was just one church in Scotland and it was in communion with the Bishop of Rome, the Pope. Within this

Church there were shades of opinion, such as the seventh century clash between the Roman and Celtic parts of the Church and the question of whether Scotland (without an Archbishop until 1472) was subject to the oversight of an Archbishop in England - a question settled by the Pope in 1192 who declared Scotland's Church "a special daughter....subject only to the Bishop of Rome".

Eventually, however, the "shades" deepened into divisions, which led to the Reformation and, in 1560, the emergence of separate denominations. Initially these were the Episcopal, Presbyterian and Roman Catholic Churches and of them the Episcopalians and Presbyterians have each at times been called *The Church of Scotland.*

The name continues for the Presbyterian Church to this day while in the Episcopal Church it was used for nearly three hundred years, well into the nineteenth century, and was followed, for just ten years, by *The Protestant Episcopal Church in Scotland*, then *The Episcopal Church in Scotland* and currently *The Scottish Episcopal Church.*

The word "Reformation" covers a wide series of changes in Western Christianity between the 14th and 17th centuries. It began with John Wycliffe (1329-84), an English philosopher and priest, who argued that the Pope's claims were not founded in Scripture. The Lollards and Hussites in Europe took his views further and, although successive Popes regained authority, discontent continued to simmer. In Germany Martin Luther (1483-1546), the Vicar-General of eleven Augustinian monasteries, began to teach that faith alone and not works is the ground for justification before God. In Switzerland Ulrich Zwingli (1484-1531) and John Calvin (1509-64) carried through anti-papal, anti-hierarchic and anti-monastic reforms and promulgated a completely new theology.

The situation in England was complicated by King Henry VIII's desire to extend the sovereign's power into every area of English life, eventually including the overthrow of rivals such as the authority of the Pope and the power and influence of monastic houses. It came to a point of crisis in 1527 when Henry, anxious about the future of the Tudor dynasty, wished to divorce Catherine of Aragon and re-marry. The divorce was refused by Pope Clement VII and Henry then broke with Rome and declared the Church of England to be the established Church in the land, with himself as its Supreme Governor.

In Scotland the Reformation had a different catalyst to the one in England. The early death of James IV left the crown to his seventeen month old son, James V, and the care of the kingdom to a succession of Regents (including James IV's widow, Margaret Tudor, and Archibald Douglas, 6th Earl of Angus, who married the widowed Queen. (Estranged from her, he kept the young king a virtual prisoner while governing in his name until James, aged fourteen, escaped, and the Earl went into exile.)

On New Year's Day 1537 the twenty-four year old James V married Madeleine of Valois, the sixteen year old daughter of King Francis I of France. However, the new Queen was already ill with tuberculosis and died seven months later. Within a year James married another Frenchwoman, the twenty-three year old Mary of Guise and Lorraine, daughter of one French Duke and widow of another. James and Mary had three children but two of them, James and Robert, died in infancy and when the king himself died at the age of thirty, soon after a Scottish defeat at the Battle of Solway Moss, his six day old daughter became Mary, Queen of Scots. The Crown had again come to a child and, as before, power to a succession of Regents. There were attempts from both England and France to secure the future marriage of the infant Queen and - as elsewhere in Europe - an increasing interest in Reformed theology.

A leading advocate of Scottish Reform, and certainly the best known, was John Knox. He was born in East Lothian in, most probably, 1514, the year after Flodden's battle, educated at St Andrews University and ordained as a priest in 536. However, his thinking was guided by the work of the early Reformers, men like George Wishart, and, after the murder, by a group of Reformers, of the Archbishop of St Andrews, Cardinal David Beaton, in the Castle at St Andrews in 1547, he joined them to try and defend the castle against the French forces besieging it.

Following the fall of the castle John Knox became a prisoner in France. On his release in 1549 he travelled to England, became a priest in the Church of England and Court Preacher to Henry VIII's son, Edward VI. He had an influence on the formation of the Book of Common Prayer, which was being overseen by the Archbishop of Canterbury, Thomas Cranmer. But when Edward died, aged fifteen, and his Roman Catholic, elder half-sister Mary came to the throne John Knox moved to Geneva, where he was influenced by the teaching of John Calvin. Later, in Frankfurt, he ministered to an English refugee congregation until differences over the Liturgy ended his association with the Church of England.

John Knox returned to Scotland in 1559, answering a call from Protestant aristocrats who disliked the government of Mary of Guise, who had become Regent five years earlier. Within weeks of John Knox's arrival a proclamation banned anyone from preaching or administering the Sacraments without authority from a bishop. This was ignored by the Reformers and John Knox preached in Saint John's Church, Perth. Afterwards a priest began to say Mass and fighting began among the congregation. The outcome was the destruction of much of the interior of the church and during the next two days three monasteries in Perth were also destroyed. It was the beginning of the end for monastic life in mediaeval Scotland. It would not be restored until the 19th century.

Parliament went on to abolish the Pope's authority in Scotland (although questions remain over the legality of this as the Acts of Parliament were not accepted by the Crown – the young Queen Mary consistently declining to do so) and John Knox, in the newly called General Assembly of the Church, helped write a Confession of Faith and the first "Book of Discipline".

However, as John Knox used a prayer book and accepted bishops, modern Presbyterianism descends more from the pattern advocated by Andrew Melville. His father, the Laird of Baldovie, was killed at the Battle of Pinkie Cleugh, fought as part of Henry VIII's "Rough Wooing" in his attempt to secure the marriage of his son Edward to Mary, Queen of Scots, and so Andrew Melville's childhood was spent at his older brother's home, The Manse of Maryton. He then studied at Saint Mary's College, St Andrews, and at the University of Paris. Later he taught at Geneva, became Principal of Glasgow University, Principal of Saint Mary's College, St Andrews, and Rector of the University. He took a leading role in devising the constitution for the Presbyterian Church in the "Second Book of Discipline". He had disagreements with King James VI and I and, after four years of imprisonment in London, was refused permission to return to Scotland. For the last eleven years of his life he was Professor of Divinity at the Huguenot Academy of Sedan in France.

Chapter 2
Episcopalian - the enduring appeal.

Why did people in Scotland choose to be part of the Episcopal Church? At the Reformation many did. At the Revolution most of the country was Episcopalian, and some stayed faithful to their Church through the years of persecution and difficulties. Why?

In the 16th century Reformation thinking was found largely among clergy who had questions about the authority of the Pope and also among some of the nobility, who greatly disliked the government of the Regent, Mary of Guise, mother of Mary, Queen of Scots, and who thus had political as well as religious motives.

When Presbyterianism was first established as the Church of Scotland in 1560 there were only a handful of ministers of the new thinking and so in many places the old ways continued. In the Highlands people followed the lead of clan chiefs - if the chief was an Episcopalian then so were most, if not all, of the clan. And, of course, in parts of Scotland, notably Buchan in the north-east, there was the splendid quality of thrawn-ness. People would not be told by king or government which church they should be part of.

In the 19th century the lifting of restrictions and penalties on Episcopalians led to a boom in church building across the nation. Most of the buildings belonging to the Church at the Revolution were now in Presbyterian hands and so a new building programme began. The resurgence of the Church coincided with the Oxford Movement, which sought to recall the richness of worship in the pre-Reformation Church. The Episcopal Church had a high doctrine of the Eucharist, although its practice had been ascetic and simple. At the restoration of Episcopacy in 1660 it would have been difficult to distinguish Episcopalian and Presbyterian. Both groups of clergy wore black gowns and the only difference in worship was the Episcopalian introduction of the doxology, the Lord's Prayer and, at baptisms, the Apostles' Creed. But now a change began to happen in the Episcopal Church, both in the architecture of buildings and in the worship itself where, gradually, the celebration of the Eucharist became the normal and central act of each congregation's Sunday.

The Episcopal Church was becoming fashionable once more. Many of the nobility and gentry, educated in English public schools, felt more at home with Episcopalianism than with the Presbyterian forms of the Church of Scotland. And, in what were still autocratic times, some insisted that their household staff and estate workers were in Church with them (a practice which in a few places persisted into the 1970s). In other parts of Scotland, though, the Episcopal Church reached out to the poorest of the poor. In Dundee Bishop Forbes visited those living in the slum tenement housing in times of epidemic when others stayed away. In Aberdeen and Inverness, churches in the Anglo-Catholic tradition were founded specifically to minister to the poor, and they brought love, colour and vibrancy into the grey and harsh lives of those around them. A third element of growth came about through the greater mobility of the population and the immigration into Scotland of people whose background had been in the Anglican Churches of England, Wales, Ireland and elsewhere. It all made for the eclectic mix which is today's Scottish Episcopal Church.

Chapter 3
A Background to Reformation and Revolution

In the mid 16th century as the impending Reformation loomed over Scotland, as over much of Europe, there were two distinct groups of Reformers within Scotland – an extreme Protestant party and also a more moderate group who, though well aware of the need for change, wished to keep as much as was good of the old Church.

The efforts made by the moderate Reformers can be traced through the proceedings of the Provincial Councils and, at the last of them in 1559, there were requests that the nobility and gentry in each diocese should have a part in the election of a bishop and for parishioners to have a voice in the choice of each parish priest. These requests were put aside and the Council adjourned until the next year. Events overtook the plans, however. A crisis was brewing. Mary, Queen of Scots, married the Dauphin Francis, who soon became King of France, while in England the Roman Catholic Queen Mary died to be succeeded by her Protestant half-sister, Elizabeth.

Mary, Queen of Scots, had a claim to the English Crown through her great-grandfather, Henry VII of England, and questions persisted, at least in Roman Catholic minds, as to Elizabeth's legitimacy. It depended on whether Henry VIII's parting from Catherine of Aragon and subsequent marriage to Anne Boleyn could be considered valid. Francis I of France and Mary, Queen of Scots, made up their minds and included the Arms of England in their Coat of Arms.

In Scotland in 1557 a group of nobles – the Lords of the Congregation – encouraged Reformation preachers and there were attacks on church buildings and property. In January 1559, the anonymous *Beggars' Summons* threatened monks with eviction from their monasteries in favour of beggars. There were particular complaints about the way of life in monastic houses and this was a first, and calculated, attempt to involve the people (rather than just the nobles) in unrest. The Regent, Mary of Guise, summoned the reformed preachers to come to her at Stirling but this provoked further trouble. Armed men from Angus assembled in Dundee to accompany the preachers to Stirling, and on May 4th they were joined by John Knox, who had been invited by the Protestant nobles to return to Scotland.

Elizabeth of England offered support to the Lords of the Congregation and the Regent called on French troops. An English fleet arrived in the Firth of Forth and was followed by an army marching north. The Regent retreated to Edinburgh Castle, became ill and died on June 11th 1560, aged forty-five. A month later, under the Treaty of Edinburgh, the French and English troops withdrew.

The triumph of the extreme reformers was total, as was the failure of the moderates. The Scottish Parliament decreed the removal of the Pope's authority in Scotland and forbade the Mass. However, only forty Reformed ministers were available for over a thousand parishes, and even twelve years later, when a form of Episcopacy was restored, the number had increased to just two hundred and fifty-seven.

The next twenty years saw division. Andrew Melville, a much firmer Presbyterian than John Knox, opposed the policies advocated by the bishops and, in the end, defeated them. In 1592 Presbyterianism was formally established as the Church of Scotland, although two thirds of parishes still did not have a

Presbyterian minister. In many parts of Scotland the Reformation was regarded as a distant quarrel among the aristocracy and those adhering to the old ways continued to worship, openly or secretly depending on local circumstances.

The enforced abdication of Mary, Queen of Scots, and her years of imprisonment in England, left the Crown once more to an infant – James VI. However, the child grew and by 1600 it was clear to him that the logical conclusion of extreme Reform was the establishment of a power base able to challenge the Throne itself. So, when James succeeded Elizabeth I in 1604 and became King of England too, it was only a matter of time before the wheel turned. In 1606 the Scots Parliament removed restrictions on the office of bishop and Andrew Melville became a prisoner in the Tower of London. The General Assembly of 1610 restored full Episcopacy.

Trouble had not gone away, however, and the high-handed actions of Charles I did much to irritate almost everyone. In 1637 the king imposed a Prayer Book on Scotland without consultation with either the General Assembly or even all of the bishops. The following year the Assembly ignored the Royal Commissioner's attempt to dissolve it and deposed all the bishops, excommunicating eight of them.

However, when the English Parliament executed Charles I in 1649 the Scottish Parliament proclaimed Charles II as king. It was not until 1660, however, that the monarchy was restored in both Scotland and England, and with it came once more the establishment of the Episcopal Church as the Church of Scotland.

Charles II was - whenever it suited him - sympathetic to the claims of Presbyterianism, determined to re-establish Episcopalianism, and in secret a Roman Catholic. His personal charm somehow enabled him to get away with it. No such luck attended his brother, the Duke of York, who succeeded him as James VII and II in 1685. James was openly a Roman Catholic and established the Jesuits at Holyrood. His reign was brought to an end, however, by trouble in England. The Archbishop of Canterbury and seven other bishops were charged with seditious libel and imprisoned in the Tower of London. Their acquittal brought great rejoicing and James promised to uphold the Episcopal nature of both the Church of England and the Church of Scotland. It was too little too late and James fled to France as his son-in-law, Prince William of Orange, invaded England.

William and his wife Mary, James's daughter, were proclaimed king and queen and in England bishops, clergy and people generally welcomed them. The new monarchs would clearly have found it easier and beneficial to have the same religious settlement in England and Scotland, but the Scottish bishops - regarding the new regime as transitional and temporary - declined to break the oaths of loyalty they had made to James. And so the Presbyterian Church, for whom the oaths presented no such difficulty, again became the Church of Scotland.

In Glasgow and the west many Episcopal clergy were "rabbled" out of their churches and homes while elsewhere priests continued blithely on. One such was Michael Fraser, who was appointed priest of Daviot and Dunlichity in the Scottish Highlands in 1672. He ignored attempts by the bishop to censure him and when the bishop himself was removed in 1689 he equally ignored every attempt by the Presbytery to call him to account. His parishioners, on one occasion, sending away the Presbytery's representatives in a hail of stones. He died, still - of course - in office, in 1725, after fifty-three years of ministry in his parish.

It was Episcopalian involvement in the Jacobite Risings which caused the Church to become what Sir Walter Scott described as "a shadow of a shade". After the failure of the Risings there were penalties for Episcopalian priests who would not swear allegiance to the Hanoverian monarchs, who succeeded Queen Anne, the last Stuart to reign in person, and penalties for lay people who chose to remain loyal to the Church. A strain of "Qualified Chapels", Episcopalian in name and using the Church of England Prayer Book, also attracted some people away from the Scottish Church. The penalties on the Church were gradually relaxed during the reign of George III and removed in 1792. But by then there were just four bishops and forty priests ministering to five percent of Scotland's population.

The death of the last Stuart king-in-exile, Henry IX and I, who was a Roman Catholic Cardinal Bishop, in 1788 paved the way for a rapprochement with the Government. And the far-seeing Primus, John Skinner, also found a way in 1804 of uniting the old Non-Juring and the Qualified parts of the Church into one. The way was clear for the 19th century's growth and expansion.

But the detailed story begins in the 16th century with the Battle of Flodden in 1513. In it much of the leadership of Scotland died alongside James IV......had it remained in place would the years which followed and the Reformation in Scotland have taken a different course?

Chapter 4
The 16th Century

In which two Scottish kings die young and Mary, Queen of Scots, marries three times, abdicates and is executed. In the Church, a Cardinal is murdered and the Reformation begins.

A Moment in the Century
Flodden

Flodden - the Scots were on Branxton Hill, behind the Cross. A deep valley divided the two armies

The Battle of Flodden on September 9th 1513 is often seen as a simple defeat of the Scottish army by an English one. That is, of course, exactly what happened - but the implications of the battle go much deeper. In the late 15th century the economics and politics of the western edge of Europe were dominated equally by France, England and Scotland. They were powerful and strong nations and had a pattern of shifting alliances.

The defeat at Flodden removed both James IV, an educated and cultured Renaissance king, respected throughout Europe, and also the powerful military forces he had so carefully developed. It ended Scotland's role as a major nation in mediaeval Europe and, ever since, Scotland has struggled to avoid being dominated by England. The current conversations about the United Kingdom being stronger together mask this struggle.

The beginning of the United Kingdom has its roots in the succession of the Scottish King James VI to the throne of England and Ireland. James ruled the two kingdoms in a personal union and kept them separate. It was not until 1707 that the Union of the Parliaments was agreed, predictably amid considerable controversy in Scotland.

But in 1513 Scotland, England and France were all strong nations. The French king and the Pope asked for Scotland's help in the Europe wide *War of the Holy League*, in which England and France were on opposite sides. It was a difficult moment for James. He was married to Margaret Tudor, sister of Henry VIII of England, and had obligations to Henry under the Treaty of Perpetual Peace which he had signed before his marriage, while - on the other hand - Scotland had an affinity with France and James thought of the office of Pope as deserving considerable respect. He decided to try and distract Henry from his invasion of France by marching across the Border, just across the Border that is.

Having generously given Henry considerable notice of his intentions, James ordered his men to assemble at Edinburgh or, if more convenient, at Ellem Kirk in Berwickshire, bringing with them supplies for forty days. Around 30,000 answered the call - it was the largest army Scotland had ever gathered. A deeply pious man, James rode north to Ross-shire to pray at the Shrine of Saint Duthac at Tain before joining his army.

In Edinburgh James's men came to the Burghmuir - an area which now has the Meadows at its northern end and West Morningside and Mayfield at its southern boundary. In the 16th century this was a place very different from the genteel ambience of today – a haunt of vagrants and the city's quarantine area in time of plague. There was rough grassland, with outcrops of ancient forest, and James used it as a place to fly his hawks. In 1507 he had built the Chapel of Saint Roque on the Muir and this chapel was the focal point for the muster which began on August 13th 1513.

The king's heaviest guns left Edinburgh Castle on August 17th, each pulled by a team of thirty-two oxen, although the biggest gun of all, Mons Meg, was deemed too heavy to move. The lighter guns followed two days later with the main body of the army. The route was through Dalkeith and across the countryside to the Lammermuir Hills. At Ellem Kirk the king met those who had journeyed from Aberdeenshire, Angus, Fife and East Lothian. The whole army crossed the River Tweed near Coldstream on August 22nd and the invasion of a small corner of England began - as did the rain that was to play a crucial role in the days ahead.

The king's guns pounded Norham Castle for six days until its Constable surrendered on August 29th. The army then advanced a little further into England, capturing the castles at Wark and Etal. Ford Castle was also surrendered by its castellan, Lady Elizabeth Heron. James remained at Ford until September 5th. Legend – but not actual history – claims that the king lingered at Ford because he was enthralled by the beautiful Lady Elizabeth.

A sensible course might now have been for the army to return to Scotland. James had achieved his strategic objective of a diversion, although such a withdrawal might have encouraged an incursion into Scotland by the force which the seventy year old Earl of Surrey was hurrying north. James decided to fight and, as was the custom, Heralds from both sides arranged the place of battle and the date by which it would be fought. The rain which had been falling since the Scots crossed into England was making conditions difficult for both armies, but James prepared a magnificent defensive position on Flodden Hill. He set great store by his guns and time and care was taken to ensure that they were properly dug in to fire accurately at the approach from the south which Lord Surrey would take.

However, the English did not oblige. Lord Surrey saw that Flodden Hill, with its guns, was practically impregnable and, by dint of a gruelling two day march in appalling weather, was able to bypass Flodden and come on the Scots from the north, cutting off any option of a last minute retreat to Scotland. James hurriedly moved his guns and his army from Flodden Hill to Branxton Hill, more than a mile away and with Scotland visible behind the English army. There was no time to prepare proper gun positions and this had a devastating effect on the outcome of the battle. When fighting began in the late afternoon the recoil of the king's guns was not contained by the hurriedly constructed gun positions and the shot went over the heads of the English army. The battle would be decided by close combat – and the rain. James had confidence in the effectiveness of a new weapon - eighteen foot long pikes - and so his advance began.

In hindsight James should have waited in his new positions on Branxton Hill and allowed the English to attack up the steep slope. But the English gunners, with much lighter field guns, were not having the difficulties which the Scots gunners experienced and were finding their targets. James began the advance down the hill. His army was larger than the English and equipped with his new pikes, which were much longer than the English billhooks. It was crucial for the battle plan that the divisions of pikemen held together. This worked well on the left flank where the Earls of Home and Huntly's men had firm ground and the English, commanded by Edmund Howard, Lord Surrey's son, were routed. Only an intervention by cavalry saved the English from early defeat.

Soon, however, the tables were turned. The division led by three Earls - Erroll, Crawford and Montrose - was having a difficult time. A stream, unseen from the top of Branxton Hill, was swollen by the rain and the area around it was a sea of liquid mud. The long pikes became unmanageable as their bearers sank up to their knees in mud, while the shorter English billhooks and arrows from the bowmen proved more effective in such circumstances. A similar fate befell the king's own division, which he led in person from the front.

When James saw that defeat was inevitable he made a personal charge at the Earl of Surrey himself. No one doubted his bravery as he was cut down within a few yards of his quarry. Seeing the king die many in his army made their escape, south to England and then back by other roads home. Others, though, fought loyally on. The killing continued until around 7 O'Clock when darkness began to fall. In total 10,000 Scots died, a third of the army. The English dead were around 1500. It was the last mediaeval battle to be fought in England. Muskets and pistols would soon replace the pikes, billhooks, spears and arrows used on Branxton Hill.

The next day King James's body was identified - like most of the others who fell it had been stripped naked overnight by looters. The body was placed in the chancel of Branxton Church, wrapped in what remained of the Royal Standard, and it was later embalmed at Berwick-upon-Tweed. The Earl of Surrey escorted the body to London but it is uncertain what happened to it there. Some say that the king was buried in an unmarked grave at Saint Michael's, Cornhill (a church destroyed in the Great Fire of London and rebuilt by Christopher Wren) while others claim that the embalmed body was taken to the Carmelite monastery at Sheen, close to Henry VIII's palace at Richmond, to await Henry's return from France, and from there disappeared into the mists of unknown history.

But, whatever happened to his body, Scotland's Renaissance king was dead, aged forty. He had reigned since he was fifteen. A pious man, frequently on pilgrimage, who built many churches and who could speak a variety of languages – Lowland Scots, Gaelic, English, French, Italian, German, Flemish, Danish and Latin. A king who was often depressed and who gambled heavily but who also encouraged the arts and science. A king fascinated by warfare, not only acquiring a formidable array of artillery for Scotland's army but also strengthening the navy, including building the *Michael*, the biggest warship anywhere of its day. A king who fathered eleven children – six with Queen Margaret, of whom only the future James V survived infancy, and five by four other women. The oldest of these children, Alexander Stewart, Archbishop of St Andrews, died with his father at Flodden.

James was succeeded by his son, who was eighteen months old. He was crowned as James V at Stirling on September 21st, twelve days after the battle. He lived a difficult and eventful life. Like his father he clashed with Henry VIII and was defeated by the English at the Battle of Solway Moss on November 24th 1542. He returned north to Linlithgow and Falkland Palaces and died, aged thirty, three weeks later, on December 14th 1542. His death came six days after his daughter Mary was born - Mary, Queen of Scots, mother to James VI who also became King James I of England and Ireland and thereby established the first personal union of the two kingdoms.

The Chronological Story of the 16th Century

1513 Scotland's Renaissance King, James IV, dies in the Battle of Flodden and with him many of the leaders of Church and State.

1517 Martin Luther publishes Ninety-Five Theses, a significant moment in the long process known as the Reformation

1521 The Pope designates King Henry VIII of England as Defender of the Faith – a title retained by British monarchs to this day.

1525 The Scottish Parliament forbids the circulation of books by Martin Luther which question the Pope's authority.

1528 Patrick Hamilton, formerly Precentor of the Cathedral at St Andrew's, becomes the first martyr of the Reformation – being burned at the stake in St Andrews on the orders of Archbishop James Beaton – for supporting Martin Luther's teaching.

1537 King James V marries Madeleine of Valois, daughter of the French king, Francis I, but she dies seven months later.

1538 King James V marries the twenty-three year old Mary of Guise, widow of Louis d'Orleans, Duc de Longueville. (Henry VIII of England sought to marry her immediately after Louis' death in 1537).

1542 King James V dies and is succeeded by his six day old daughter, Mary, Queen of Scots. The Earl of Arran, next in line to the throne after the infant Queen, is appointed Governor of the Kingdom and a marriage treaty is arranged with Henry VIII under which Mary should eventually marry Henry's son, Edward. Cardinal David Beaton begins reform of the Church through provincial councils, introduces a catechism in Scots and encourages preaching which engages with the people.

1544 George Wishart, a graduate of King's College, Aberdeen, and a former schoolmaster at Montrose, becomes an itinerant preacher, travelling through Scotland preaching the Reformation.

1546 George Wishart is arrested and burnt to death outside St Andrews Castle as Cardinal Beaton watches from a window. Two months later the Castle is seized by Reformers and the Cardinal murdered. The castle is re-taken by French troops and John Knox, who had joined its defenders, is captured and sent as a prisoner to France. On his release he goes to England, becomes a priest in the Church of England and a Chaplain to King Edward VI. He is offered, but declines, the Bishopric of Rochester.

1546 Mary of Guise, mother of Mary, Queen of Scots, resists English pressure for a future marriage of her daughter to Edward, son of Henry VIII.

1547 King Henry VIII of England dies and is succeeded by Edward VI, Henry's son by Jane Seymour, his third wife. As the new king is just ten years old his uncle, the Duke of Somerset, is designated as Lord Protector.

1548 Five year old Mary, Queen of Scots, travels to France where she is brought up with the French royal children, with the intention that she ultimately marries the Dauphin (heir to the French throne), Francis.

1549 The first English Book of Common Prayer is published, with Thomas Cranmer as its principal author.

1552 The second English Book of Common Prayer is published.

1553 Edward VI of England dies, aged sixteen. An attempt to make Lady Jane Grey the Queen fails and Mary, daughter of Henry VIII and Catherine of Aragon, becomes Queen. John Knox leaves England for Geneva and then Frankfurt. Roman Catholicism is restored in England and in 1556 three Anglican bishops - Thomas Cranmer, Archbishop of Canterbury; Nicholas Ridley, Bishop of London; and Hugh Latimer, Bishop of Worcester - are burnt as heretics.

1554 The Queen Dowager, Mary of Guise, becomes Regent of Scotland.

1558 Queen Mary of England and Ireland dies and is succeeded by her half-sister, Elizabeth, daughter of Henry VIII and Anne Boleyn, Henry's second wife. The Church of England is re-established with the monarch as its Supreme Governor. Mary, Queen of Scots, lays claim to the English throne as great-granddaughter of Henry VII of England.

1558 Sixteen year old Mary, Queen of Scots, marries the heir to the French throne, the Dauphin Francis, who is just over a year younger than her. A secret treaty is signed which will make Scotland part of France should she die without an heir.

1559 Francis becomes King Francis II of France and Mary the Queen Consort of France as well as Queen of Scots.

1559 The third English Book of Common prayer is published.

1559 The Regent, Mary of Guise, treats Reformers with severity and John Knox, imbued with Calvinist theology, returns to Scotland at the request of some of the Protestant nobles. The Regent requests help from France and the Protestants receive aid from England. On the approach of an English army Mary of Guise takes refuge in Edinburgh Castle and dies there, aged forty-five. A month later the Treaty of Edinburgh is agreed and French troops leave Scotland.

1560 The Scottish Parliament removes the Pope's authority in Scotland, forbids the Mass and restricts the administration of Sacraments to those admitted as preachers. The legality of the Acts is uncertain as the young Queen Mary constantly declines to ratify them. The General Assembly of the Church comes into being, with both Ministers and Lay Commissioners as members. "Superintendents" replace bishops. The Roman wing of the Church is never again the "Established" Church of Scotland and for almost three hundred years the word "Bishop" almost always refers to those in what becomes the Episcopal Church. It was not until 1848 that bishops were once more resident in Roman Catholic Dioceses in Scotland.
The pre-Reformation bishops made no attempt to continue the Apostolic Succession of Bishops and several, including the Bishops of Caithness, Orkney and Galloway, joined the Reformers and continued to have authority in their former

dioceses. Of the two archbishops the Archbishop of Glasgow was the Ambassador to France in 1560 and remained there until his death forty-three years later. The Archbishop of St Andrews, John Hamilton, brother of the Earl of Arran, the former Regent, went through difficult days. He was imprisoned in 1563 and after his release was an active supporter of Mary. He baptised her infant son, James, and pronounced her divorce from the Earl of Bothwell. He was present at the Battle of Langside, which ended Mary's hopes of regaining the Crown. A kinsman murdered the Regent, the Earl of Moray, in 1570 and the Archbishop was executed at Stirling the following year. On Apostolic Succession it may be noted that Patrick Forbes, Bishop of Aberdeen from 1618 to 1635, thought of this as having three forms - either an unbroken succession of Presbyters (which he regarded as the basic form); or an unbroken succession of Bishops; or the unbroken succession of saints, those individuals who, in every generation, handed on the precious truth of God (whatever the institutional Church might be doing).

1560 King Francis II of France, husband of Mary, Queen of Scots, dies aged sixteen.

1561 Mary returns to Scotland nine months after her husband's death. She is eighteen.

1562 Sir William Maitland travels to England to seek a better relationship between the Kingdoms and to assert Mary's right of succession to Queen Elizabeth.

1563 Elizabeth suggests a marriage between Mary and the Earl of Leicester.

1565 Mary marries Henry Stewart, Earl of Darnley. Both are Roman Catholics and the Queen resolves to attempt the restoration of the Roman Catholic Church, although her husband advises against it.

1566 James, the future King James VI and I, is born in Edinburgh Castle.

1567 The Earl of Darnley is murdered and Mary marries the Earl of Bothwell in a Protestant ceremony. Later she surrenders herself to the nobles and consents to the abolition of cathedral services throughout Scotland. While imprisoned at Loch Leven Castle she nominates her half-brother, the Earl of Moray, as Regent for her infant son and then abdicates. She never sees her child again. The thirteen month old James becomes James VI of Scotland, crowned at Stirling by Adam Bothwell, Bishop of Orkney, who had joined the Reformers in 1560.

1568 Mary escapes from Loch Leven Castle and within a few days gathers an army of 6000. Her abdication and consent to the coronation of her son are declared to have been obtained under threat of death and are thus invalid. A document demanding her restitution is signed by nine bishops, twelve abbots, eight earls, eighteen lords and almost a hundred barons. Mary watches the defeat of her army, commanded by the Earl of Argyll, at the Battle of Langside. She travels to Dundrennan Abbey, sixty miles away in Galloway, and from there crosses the Solway Firth to England where she is held prisoner for nineteen years.

1571 The Thirty-Nine articles of Religion are agreed by the English Parliament

1572 The Episcopate, abolished in 1560, is restored at the Convention of Leith. John Knox supports the move, although bishops are now appointed, rather than consecrated, and are subject to the General Assembly.

1584 The sixteen year old James VI makes an attempt at reconciliation with his grandmother's family in France and with the Pope.

1587 Mary, Queen of Scots, is beheaded at Fotheringay Castle in Lincolnshire, after nineteen years of imprisonment in England. Queen Elizabeth maintains that she had not intended an execution.

1589 James VI marries the fifteen year old Anne of Denmark, daughter of King Frederick II of Denmark and Norway.

1592 Presbyterianism is established as the Church of Scotland although the titular, appointed, bishops continue to sit in parliament. New "bishops", known as "Commissioners" are appointed to vacant bishoprics as King James VI realises that Presbyterianism is likely to challenge the throne itself - Andrew Melville, a leading reformer, has said that there are two kingdoms in Scotland and one is the Kirk. In this kingdom James cannot be a King, or Head, but only a member.

Another Moment in the Century
Castle of Martyrdom and Murder

The Castle of St Andrews

St Andrews' Castle was the home of the Bishops and Archbishops of St Andrews and the scene of much violence during the Reformation. The first castle was probably built around 1200 but the present ruins show much subsequent development. George Wishart, a Reformation martyr, accused of heresy, was burned alive in the street outside the castle gate in March 1546. Two months later, in reprisal, Protestant nobles and their retinue seized the castle and Cardinal David Beaton, Archbishop of St Andrews, was murdered. His body was hung from a window, possibly the one from which he had watched George Wishart die. The castle withstood a year long seige from the Regent, the Earl of Arran, but eventually fell to French troops, assisted by a French fleet off-shore. John Knox, ordained a priest eleven years earlier, joined the Reformers holding the Castle in May

1547, shortly before its fall, and, as a result, spent two years as a French prisoner.

Saint Andrews had gradually gained a dominant place in the life of the Church. The importance of the old Celtic centre on Iona had been eroded when Viking raids in 849 forced the removal of the saint's remains to a safer resting place. St Andrews had the advantage of possessing relics of Andrew the Apostle, which became a useful tool in fending off the claims of English archbishops to jurisdiction over the Scottish Church.

In 1144 life in St Andrews was enhanced by the establishment of a Community of Augustinian Canons. It meant though that the existing clergy, the Culdees, were displaced, eventually finding a home in the most easterly of the churches in the town. This Church of Saint Mary-on-the-Rock was on a rocky promontory, overlooking the harbour and just outside the precinct walls of, what was to become, the Cathedral. Only the foundations and first courses of the walls of Saint Mary-on-the-Rock still stand.

The Augustinians based themselves in Saint Rule's Church, which dates from about 1130. It was extended in 1144 to accommodate the Canons. Today all that remains of Saint Rule's is a small part of the Chancel and the 100 foot tower. It is possible to climb the steps inside it and from the top there are views over all of St Andrews.

By 1160 it was clear that even the enlarged Saint Rule's was too small and the building of the largest cathedral in Scotland began. The work took nearly 150 years to complete and the Cathedral was consecrated on July 5th 1318 in the presence of King Robert the Bruce.

Down the centuries the Cathedral was battered by storms and gales but it was the wind of change that was the Reformation which did the real damage. On June 11th 1559 John Knox, back in St Andrews, preached a sermon which so aroused people that they went to the Cathedral and destroyed all that the Reformers described as "Popery". The Canons may, or may not, have had time to hide the relics of Andrew the Apostle. The relics disappeared that day and have not been seen since. A plaque in the Cathedral ruins marks the place where the Shrine of Andrew once stood. The Church of Saint Mary-on-the-Rock was also destroyed, probably in the first wave of attacks on June 11th. The Cathedral and its monastery ceased to function on June 14th and within a week all the Augustinian Canons had left the town.

Today all that remains of the great Cathedral are fragments - a large part of the Precinct wall is still in place as are parts of the west gable, facing the old town's two main streets, a wall of the nave and the east gable.

The west doorway of St Andrews Cathedral and the east gable

Chapter 5
THE 17th Century

In which James VI of Scotland becomes also James I of England. The Episcopal Church becomes the Church of Scotland again - and then, once more, isn't.

A Moment in the Century
The Honours of Scotland

Dunnottar Castle, near Stonehaven Photo: Dick Davis.

South from Aberdeen is the Howe of the Mearns, a place which inspired saints but into whose red earth the blood of kings drained.

The Howe forms much of ancient Kincardineshire and early Scotland was ruled from the castle-palace which guarded the route to the north via Cairn O'Mount. The palace was at Fettercairn, but nothing of it now remains. Its builder, King Malcolm II, died in 954, at Fetteresso, another Mearns royal castle. Later two other kings met violent deaths in the Howe -

Kenneth II was murdered at Fettercairn and Duncan II, a few miles away at Mondynes.

Coming south from Aberdeen the coast road passes Stonehaven and Catterline before a by-road leads off towards the sea. This ends at the Old Church of Kinneff. No longer in regular use - but open each day – the church welcomes visitors with its story.

Saint Adamnan, a monk of Iona, travelled along the east coast of Scotland in the seventh century and he chose the tree-lined cleft, leading inland from the sea-cliffs, as a site of one of the churches he founded on his journey. There has been a church at Kinneff ever since. Although the present church building dates from a 1738 renovation, it is built on the foundations of its predecessor. The site of Adamnan's cell is also sometimes pointed out close by - under the steading of the former Manse.

Kinneff played a role in Scotland's 17th century troubles. In 1652 the Royalist armies had been defeated and Dunnottar Castle, seven miles up the coast from Kinneff, was besieged by the English Parliamentary army and about to surrender. Within the castle were the Honours of Scotland, the crown jewels.

Just before the castle's surrender, the wife of the minister of Kinneff, Christian Grainger, charmed Cromwell's general into allowing her into the castle to visit her friend, the wife of Dunnottar's governor. Mrs Grainger left with the crown jewels concealed about her person and the Sceptre and Sword of State wrapped in a cloth. The courteous Major-General Morgan even helped her onto her horse for the journey back to Kinneff, where the Honours were concealed beneath the pulpit of the church until the restoration of King Charles II in 1660.

The Chronological Story of the 17th Century

1603 Queen Elizabeth dies in England, aged seventy, and is succeeded by King James VI, who becomes also King James I of England and Ireland. However, Scotland and England continue as separate nations with their own Parliaments and Judiciary - both nations being ruled by James in a personal union. He styles himself King of Great Britain and Ireland. He and Queen Anne are crowned at Windsor Castle.

1606 The Scottish Parliament removes restrictions placed on the office of bishop. Andrew Melville is imprisoned in the Tower of London.

1607 The first English colony is established in America. The Bishop of London is given responsibility for the Episcopal oversight of the emerging colonial church. With the victory of the United States in the American War of Independence in 1783 such an arrangement is no longer appropriate. The first bishop for the United States, Samuel Seabury, is consecrated in Aberdeen in 1784.

1610 Episcopacy in Scotland is restored at the Assembly of Glasgow and three of the titular bishops – John Spottiswood of Glasgow, Andrew Lamb of Brechin and Gavin Hamilton of Galloway - travel to London for consecration as bishops, returning to consecrate others.

1611 The King James edition of The Bible is published.

1612 Henry Frederick, James's eldest son, dies aged eighteen. The King's second son, Charles becomes heir, aged twelve.

1616 The Scottish Church establishes schools in every parish to teach children "Godliness and knowledge".

1619 Anne of Denmark, the Queen, dies, aged forty-five.

1625 James VI and I dies and is succeeded by his son, Charles I. Two months later Charles marries, by proxy, the Roman Catholic Princess Henrietta-Maria, sister of King Louis XIII of France. The vows are exchanged in person at Canterbury a year later.

1633 William Laud becomes Archbishop of Canterbury and begins a series of reforms attempting to ensure religious uniformity in England. Puritan organisations are closed and some priests removed from their posts. He opposes Calvinist thinking and demands that the Church of England's worship be that of the Book of Common Prayer and that internal architecture of English churches emphasise the Altar. To encourage acceptance of all of this the Archbishop brings those who refuse before the Court of the Star Chamber (which allows evidence obtained through torture) and the Court of High Commission (which accepts self-incriminating evidence).

1633 Charles I makes his first visit to Scotland as king and is crowned King of Scots at Holyrood. The Diocese of Edinburgh is created by the king and is to rank third after the two Archdioceses of St Andrews and Glasgow. (All the other Scottish dioceses pre-date the Reformation, although the Diocese of Galloway was part of the Province of York and the Diocese of Orkney, at various times, came under the jurisdiction of the Archbishoprics of Hamburg, York and Trondheim. Both Orkney and Galloway became officially part of the Scottish Church in 1472).

1636 A Book of Canons, and the following year, a new Prayer Book are presented in the name of King Charles I, without any consultation with the General Assembly, or indeed all of the Bishops.

1638 The National Covenant is signed by thousands of Scots. It seeks to preserve Presbyterianism in the face of Charles I's actions and intentions.

1638 Episcopacy is again abolished in Scotland by the General Assembly in response to the king's actions. The Marquess of Hamilton, the Royal Commissioner, dissolves the Assembly, but this is ignored and the Assembly deposes all fourteen bishops from ministry (excommunicating eight of them). In continuing to meet after the Commissioner's dissolution the Assembly is, effectively, in rebellion against the King.

1639 The Wars of the Covenant begin. Fighting is initially in the north east as the Marquess of Montrose, a signatory to the Covenant, occupies Aberdeen. The king's army marches north from England but a truce – the Pacification of Berwick – is agreed. The Scottish Parliament confirms the decisions made by the General Assembly in the previous year.

1640 The English army marches south and the Scots capture Newcastle. A truce is signed at Ripon with Charles I agreeing to pay the cost of keeping the Scot's army in northern England.

1641 Charles I travels to Edinburgh and confirms the decisions of the Scottish Parliament. A Roman Catholic rising in Ulster is contained with the assistance of soldiers from Scotland.

1642 The Civil Wars begin in England as the Parliament in London and the king clash. The Scots offer to support the

Parliamentary side in return for English acceptance of a "Solemn League and Covenant", which effectively makes England Presbyterian.

1644 A Scottish army of 20,000 men marches to support the Parliamentary Army in England. Charles I appoints the Marquess of Montrose (who has changed to the Royalist side along with other moderate Covenanters) as commander of the Royal army in Scotland. The Marquess wins battle after battle across Scotland, but in England the Parliamentary army and the Scottish Covenanters defeat the Royalist English army at the Battle of Marston Moor. Queen Henrietta-Maria and the Royal children leave England for France.

1645 The Parliamentary army, with Oliver Cromwell its second-in-command, wins a decisive victory over the king's army in England at the Battle of Naseby. In Scotland the Marquess of Montrose wins the Battle of Alford in Aberdeenshire and the Battle of Kilsyth and controls all Scotland for the king. However, the Scots Covenanting army returns from England and Lord Montrose is defeated near Selkirk.

1646 The king surrenders to Scottish Covenanters who are besieging Newark, and is taken to Newcastle. Charles I orders the Marquess of Montrose to disband the Royalist army in Scotland and leave the country - he travels to France.

1647 The Scottish Covenanters transfer Charles I into English custody for a payment of £200,000.

1648 A Scots army of 20,000 marches into England in support of the king after an agreement is reached between Charles I and moderate Covenanters. Oliver Cromwell defeats the Scots at Preston. He then visits Edinburgh and leaves with radical

Covenanters in power and also with an English army still in the Scots capital.

1649 Charles I is executed in London, without any consultation with the Scots. Within a week the Scottish Parliament proclaims Charles II as king and a month later the English Parliament declares England a republic. A delegation from Scotland travels to the Continent to ask Charles II to accept that all the countries of the British Isles should be Presbyterian. The king declines to do so.

1650 The Marquess of Montrose lands in Orkney on the king's behalf, but his small force of Scandinavian mercenaries and Orcadians is defeated at the Battle of Carbisdale at the Kyle of Sutherland. The Marquess is executed at Edinburgh Castle. Charles II lands at Garmouth in Morayshire and immediately signs the Covenant and Solemn League. Oliver Cromwell marches an army into Scotland and wins an early victory at the Battle of Dunbar.

1651 On New Year's Day Charles II is crowned King of Scots at Scone in Perthshire. Later he marches into England and is defeated at the Battle of Worcester. After six weeks as a fugitive in England he sails from Sussex to France.

1652 General George Monck becomes Governor of Scotland.

1652 Dunnottar Castle on the Kincardineshire coast, the last Royalist foothold in eastern Scotland, surrenders after an eight month siege. However, the Honours of Scotland - the crown jewels - are smuggled out of the castle and hidden in nearby Kinneff Church until the restoration of the monarchy in 1660.

1653 Oliver Cromwell becomes Lord Protector in England. A meeting of the General Assembly in Edinburgh is disbanded by Colonel Cotterel at the head of a military force.

1657 The "Tender of Union" gives Scotland thirty seats in a united Parliament in London. The English Parliament passed the initial declaration in 1651 and after a number of interim steps a formal Act of Union was agreed in 1657. It was repealed by both the Scottish and English Parliaments at the restoration of the monarchy in 1660.

1658 Oliver Cromwell dies and is succeeded by his son Richard, who resigns in 1659. General Monck, who had served Oliver Cromwell loyally, changes sides and marches into England from Coldstream. (Charles II later creates him Duke of Albemarle and his Regiment becomes the Coldstream Guards).

1660 Charles II, aged thirty, is restored to the throne and Episcopacy re-established in both Scotland and England.

1661 The Scottish Parliament passes the Rescissory Act, removing Presbyterian Church government and reverting to the pre-1638 position. The Episcopal Church is once more the Church of Scotland. However, of the bishops in 1638 only Thomas Sydserf, Bishop of Galloway, remains alive. He is appointed to the Diocese of Orkney and four new Scottish bishops are consecrated in Westminster Abbey by the Bishops of London, Llandaff, Worcester and Carlisle. Opposition to the king and the newly re-established Episcopalian Church of Scotland continues.

1662 The fourth Book of Common Prayer is published. It is still authorised for use within the Church of England.

1669 The Assertory Act gives Charles II supreme authority over the Church and People of Scotland.

1669 Henrietta-Maria, widow of Charles I, dies in France. She left England during the Civil War, coming back at the restoration of the monarchy in 1660 but returning to France five years later.

1670 Charles II agrees the Treaty of Dover with the French king, Louis XIV. Part of the Treaty is kept secret and, in this part, Charles agrees to declare publicly, at a suitable time, that he has become a Roman Catholic. (He receives a large sum of money from King Louis to forward this project and lessen his financial dependence on Parliament in England, but no "suitable" time appears).

1679 James Sharp, Archbishop of St Andrews, is murdered and an armed Covenanter rebellion begins. The rebels have an initial victory over a Government army at Drumclog but are finally defeated at Bothwell Brig.

1685 Charles II dies and is succeeded by his brother, James VII and II. The new king is openly a Roman Catholic. The Scottish Parliament refuses to pass a Bill favouring the Roman Church and James makes the Bill an Act of Council and establishes the Jesuits at Holyrood.

1687 The Declaration of Liberty of Conscience is issued in Scotland granting freedom of public worship to all "non-conformists" – Roman Catholics, Presbyterians and Quakers. The Declaration states that subjects are to obey the king's "sovereign authority, prerogative Royal, and absolute power without reserve", although the concept of "liberty of Grace" was ahead of the rest of 17th Century thinking.

1688 James asks that the Declaration of Liberty of Conscience be read in all churches in England. The Archbishop of Canterbury and six English bishops refuse and are imprisoned in the Tower of London, charged with seditious libel. When they are acquitted after a trial James II promises to uphold the rights of the Anglican and Episcopal Churches, but it is too late. His son-in-law, William, Prince of Orange, invades England and James flees to France. In the south-west of Scotland there is considerable disorder during the winter of 1688-89 and more than a hundred Episcopalian clergy are "rabbled" out of their churches and homes. Dean Robert Scott presents a petition to William, on behalf of the Archbishop of Glasgow and his clergy, asking for protection. William forbids all disturbance and violence, although this has little effect.

1689 A meeting in London between King William and the Bishop of Edinburgh, Alexander Rose, does not go well. The Bishop had travelled to London during the troubles of the previous year, carrying a letter of support for James VII and II from the Scottish bishops. But instead of James he meets William. The new king is willing to keep the Episcopalian form of church government in Scotland but Bishop Rose is unable to take sole responsibility for the Scottish bishops' allegiance to the new monarchs. At their meeting the King says "My Lord, are you going for Scotland?" The Bishop replies "Yes, sir, if you have any commands for me." William says "I hope you will be kind to me, and follow the example of England." The Bishop replies cautiously "I shall serve you as far as law, reason or conscience shall allow me." King William turns away without another word.

1689 A second opportunity for the Scottish bishops comes in March when the Convention of Estates, 150 members of the Three Estates (including the Archbishop of St Andrews, the

Archbishop of Glasgow and seven bishops) meets in Edinburgh.

William wishes to win the support of the Scottish bishops (as he has done with the majority of English ones). The Duke of Hamilton promises that the Episcopal Church will be secure and continue as the Church of Scotland if the bishops will give the same support to the new king and queen as the English bishops are doing. The Scottish bishops say they cannot break their oaths of allegiance to James.

Many of the Jacobites leave the Convention which then declares that James has forfeited his right to the throne. The Crown of Scotland is offered to Mary, James's eldest daughter, and her husband William. Clergy are ordered to pray for the new monarchs. In accepting the Crown William makes it clear that he intends to allow no persecution.

1689 The First Jacobite Rising begins. In April John Graham of Claverhouse, Viscount Dundee, raises King James's Standard on Dundee Law. By July he has eight battalions and two companies, almost all Highlanders. This army defeats a much larger force at the Battle of Killiecrankie on July 27th 1689 About two thousand of King William's troops die in the fighting and about six hundred Jacobite soldiers are killed, including Bonnie Dundee himself. The Battle of Dunkeld the next month ends in a Jacobite defeat. However, much of northern Scotland remains opposed to rule by William and Mary.

1689 In July a petition is received by the Estates from the Aberdeen Diocesan Synod asking for a meeting of a free General Assembly to heal division and settle the government of the Church. The Presbyterians oppose this as they would be outnumbered six to one by Episcopalians in such an Assembly.

1689 The Estates (of peers, barons and burgesses) ratifies the Westminster Confession of Faith and establishes the Presbyterian form of government of the Church. However, many Episcopal priests remain in actual charge of parish churches with the support of their people. (For example, William Dunbar - appointed to Cruden parish church after the Revolution, without taking oaths of loyalty to William and Mary - remained until removed one Sunday morning in 1718 by a troop of soldiers for his role in the 1715 Rising. The entire congregation went with him.)

The bishops are deprived of the income of their dioceses. They are slow to re-organise the Church as they consider the new settlement as provisional, and continue to look forward to the Episcopal Church being once more the established Church of Scotland.

The future of the thirteen pre-Revolution bishops (and one bishop-elect) varies. They had all been appointed under *congre d'elire* from either Charles II or James VII.

Arthur Rose was Archbishop of St Andrews, and Primate, from 1684 until his death in 1704. He had been Bishop of Argyll, Bishop of Galloway and Archbishop of Glasgow before his appointment to St Andrews. In 1689 he retired into private life, although nominally remaining Archbishop. He died in Edinburgh on June 13th 1704 and is buried at Restalrig, Leith.

John Paterson was Archbishop of Glasgow from 1687 to 1708. He had previously been Bishop of Galloway and Bishop of Edinburgh. He was imprisoned in Edinburgh Castle in 1692 and lived in London between 1695 and 1696, petitioning for permission to return to Scotland. When this was granted he moved to Edinburgh and sought to help dispossessed

Episcopal clergy. In Queen Anne's reign he visited London again and enlisted her sympathy and help. He died in Edinburgh on December 9th 1708 and is buried at Holyrood.

Alexander Rose was Bishop of Edinburgh from 1688 to 1720. His father, another Alexander Rose, was the priest at Monymusk in Aberdeenshire and his uncle was Arthur Rose, Archbishop of St Andrews. Before his appointment to Edinburgh he had previously been Professor of Divinity at Glasgow University, Principal of Saint Mary's College, St Andrews, and Bishop of Moray.

At the Revolution Bishop Rose remained in Edinburgh and continued to minister. He opened a meeting house in Carrubber's Close (a fore-runner of Old Saint Paul's Church, Edinburgh) and was the most active of the bishops. He is regarded as the first Primus of the Church, assuming the presiding role on the death of his uncle, the Archbishop of St Andrews, in 1704. He died, aged seventy-four, at his sister's house in the Canongate, Edinburgh, on March 20th 1720 and is buried at Restalrig Church, Leith.

The Bishop of Aberdeen, between 1682 and 1715, was George Haliburton. He had previously been Bishop of Brechin. At the Revolution in 1689 he retired to his estate at Denhead, Coupar Angus, in Perthshire, where he supported the Episcopal incumbent of Newtyle in resisting the appointment of a Presbyterian minister to the parish. The bishop acted as priest at Meigle from 1693 to 1705. He died at Denhead on September 29th 1715.

The Diocese of Argyll was in a vacancy in 1689. Alexander Monro, Principal of Edinburgh University, had been nominated by James VII on October 24th 1688 but had still to be consecrated as a bishop. He resigned from his ministry at

Saint Giles', Edinburgh, in April 1689 to avoid taking the Oath of Allegiance to William and Mary and the following year faced a Commission whose task was to remove "all scandalous, inefficient or disaffected persons" from Edinburgh University. He was neither scandalous nor inefficient but refused to change his political opinions and so was removed as Principal. He died in London in 1698.

The Bishop of Brechin from 1684 to 1695 was James Drummond. He had previously been the priest at Muthill in Perthshire and at the Revolution retired to Slains Castle at Cruden Bay in Aberdeenshire, the home of the Earl and Countess of Erroll. The bishop was a kinsman of Countess Anne. He was a great support to the Episcopalian incumbent of Cruden, William Dunbar, and gave two silver chalices to the church (they are still in use in the Presbyterian parish church). He also built the Bishop's Bridge over the Water of Cruden, and this too is still in use. He died on April 13th 1695 and is buried within the present parish church of Cruden.

Andrew Wood was Bishop of Caithness from 1680 to 1695. He had previously been the priest at Dunbar in East Lothian and, by Royal Prerogative, he continued to hold the incumbency as bishop. He was appointed Bishop of the Isles in 1677 and translated to Caithness in 1680. He died in Dunbar in 1695.

John Hamilton was Bishop of Dunkeld from 1686 to 1690. He had previously been Sub-Dean of the Chapel Royal and priest of the Tolbooth Church in Edinburgh. He was nominated as Bishop of Dunkeld in 1696 when Andrew Bruce was deprived of the See by James VII for opposing the king's plan to extend toleration to Roman Catholics. He died in the autumn of 1690.

The Bishop of Dunblane from 1684 to 1716 was Robert Douglas, cousin of the Duke of Hamilton. He had previously been Dean of Glasgow and then Bishop of Brechin. In 1689 he retired to Dudhope Castle, Dundee, and died on April 22nd 1716.

The Bishop of Galloway from 1688 to 1697 was John Gordon. He was born in Ellon, Aberdeenshire, and served as a Naval Chaplain and as a Chaplain to James VII. He was with James in Ireland and served as Chancellor of Dublin. He subsequently went into exile in France with James and conducted services for Protestant members of the exiled king's Court. He resigned as Bishop of Galloway in 1697 and in 1702 was re-ordained in Rome by the Pope as a Roman Catholic priest. He died in Rome in 1726, the last survivor of the pre-Revolution Bishops of Scotland.

Archibald Graham was Bishop of The Isles from 1680 to 1702. He was also incumbent of Rothesay from 1667 to 1685 and of Kingarth from 1682 to 1689. He died in Edinburgh of a fever on June 28th 1702. He left his library to the Parish of Rothesay.

William Hay was Bishop of Moray from 1688 to 1707. He had previously been Master of the Music School in Old Aberdeen (succeeding his father) and then priest of the East Church in Perth. In July 1689 (three months after most of the other bishops) he was deprived of the income of the See and retired to Inverness. He died at the house of his son-in-law, John Cuthbert of Castlehill, on March 19th 1707.

The Bishop of Orkney from 1688 to 1699 was Andrew Bruce. He had been Professor of Divinity and Rector of St Andrews University, Archdeacon of St Andrews and a Chaplain to King Charles II, who nominated him as Bishop of Dunkeld in

1679. He was deprived of that See by King James VII in 1686 as he opposed the king's intention of allowing greater freedom of worship for Roman Catholics. He became Bishop of Orkney two years later and was deprived of the income of that See eight months later. He retired to Kilrenny (his first charge from 1665 to 1671) and died there on March 18th 1699.

The Bishop of Ross from 1684 to 1696 was James Ramsay, son of the incumbent of the High Kirk of Glasgow. James Ramsay was ordained by the Presbytery of Glasgow in 1653 and became incumbent of Kirkintilloch and then of Linlithgow, where he remained after the restoration of Episcopacy in 1660. He later became incumbent of Hamilton and Dean of Glasgow. In 1673 he became Bishop of Dunblane and the following year argued for the calling of a National Synod. He was opposed in this by James Sharp, Archbishop of St Andrews, and three weeks later was moved to the Diocese of The Isles. This appointment was recalled by the Privy Council, at the command of the King, on his agreeing to live "in all becoming duty and faithfulness to his Metropolitan and brethren". In 1684 he opposed the repeal of anti-Roman Catholic Statutes. He became Bishop of Ross in 1684 and was deprived of the income of the See in 1689. He died – in considerable poverty – in Edinburgh on October 22nd 1696 and is buried in the Canongate Churchyard, Edinburgh.

1690 The first penal law - the Act of Assembly - requires all clergy to subscribe to the Westminster Confession.

1690 The Battle of Cromdale results in a Jacobite defeat and Fort William is built (on the site of a previous Cromwellian fort) as a northern base for the Government army. King William's victory over King James at the Battle of the Boyne in Ireland effectively brings an end to the Rising in Scotland, although skirmishes continue.

1691 In August William offers the Jacobite clans a pardon for their part in the Rising, if they take an oath of allegiance before January 1st 1692. Clan chiefs ask James, in exile in France, for his sanction for this. James gives it but it is mid-December before his message reaches the Highlands. Some are able to take the Oath before the year's end, and the massacre of the Episcopalian MacDonalds in Glencoe in February 1692 focuses the minds of others. By Spring 1692 the Jacobite clan chiefs have sworn allegiance to William and Mary.

1693 The second penal law – The Oath of Assurance - requires all holding office to swear that William is king in law and in fact.

1694 Queen Mary dies, aged thirty-two, and King William rules alone.

1695 The third penal law – The Act to Forbid Deprived Episcopal Clergy - prevents Episcopal clergy from conducting marriages or baptisms.

Another Moment in the Century
Glasgow Cathedral's Reformation

Glasgow's ancient cathedral is a place of quiet and tranquillity in the midst of the city. But it was not so in the century which followed the Reformation. The Reformers did not like the enormous, soaring building and so they set about making changes.

The Archbishop of Glasgow, James Beaton, travelled to France just in time to avoid the Reformation, taking with him the cathedral treasures and also the mace and charters of the University of Glasgow. He was Ambassador to France for the remainder of the reign of Mary, Queen of Scots, and for much of that of her son, James VI. He never returned to Scotland, although the mace was restored to the University in 1590. Much of the University archives and many of the Cathedral's treasures remained in France and were lost during the French Revolution in the late 18th century.

The Reformers left the Cathedral building intact externally but decided that there was space within it for two, and then three, separate churches. A wall was built across the nave and the west end of the Cathedral became the Outer High Church. A second congregation, the Inner High, worshipped in the Cathedral's Quire. In 1647 came the third congregation - the undercroft, which had housed Saint Kentigern's Shrine, was adapted for use by the Barony Church. Its congregation met there between 1647 and 1801, when a new building for the Barony was completed. The undercroft was then filled with five feet of earth and became a burial ground for the Barony congregation.

Fortunately, sense eventually prevailed and these structural changes were undone later in the 19th century. The Cathedral's stained glass windows were added in the 19th and 20th centuries and with them the Cathedral was restored to something approaching its mediaeval magnificence. It is now in the care of Historic Scotland and is home to a Presbyterian - Church of Scotland - congregation.

Chapter 6
The 18th Century

In which the Episcopal Church is persecuted for its support of the "Kings over the Water". The office of Primus is created and the Bishops quarrel among themselves.

A Moment in the Century
The Priests of Culloden

Culloden Moor - the last battle of the Jacobite Risings was fought here on April 16th 1746

The Jacobite Risings were pivotal points in the story of the Scottish Episcopal Church. From the early victory of the Jacobite army at Killicrankie through to the defeat fifty-seven years later at Culloden the fortunes of the Church were caught up with the Stuart cause.

The Episcopal Church as an entity took no part in the Jacobite Risings but that was far from the real story. Apart from the Roman Catholics involved, the majority of those seeking to restore the Stuarts to the throne were Episcopalian.

In 1689 the Jacobite force at Killiecrankie, led by John Graham of Claverhouse, Bonnie Dundee, charged with the battle cry "*King James and the Church of Scotland*" - by which was meant the Old Church of Scotland, the Episcopal Church.

The Scots in the Jacobite army in the 1715 Rising, apart from a small Roman Catholic contingent, were almost entirely Episcopalian, while some seventy per cent of Scots who joined the Prince Regent, Charles Edward Stuart,` in 1745 are thought to have been Episcopalians.

When William and Mary replaced King James VII and II in 1689, and Presbyterianism became the established church in Scotland in June 1690, many Episcopalian priests simply stayed on in their parish churches and continued to minister as if nothing had happened. Certainly that was the situation throughout most of Aberdeenshire and the Highlands, but one particular parish in the west has its own story.

In 1660 the Reverend Alexander MacCalman became the priest in Appin, a parish which at that time included Ballachullish, Duror and Glencoe. He remained there right through the Revolution of 1690 until his death in 1717. He was succeeded at Appin by another Episcopalian, the Reverend John McLauchlan. Six years later John McLauchlan acquired a new chalice and paten. On the chalice were inscribed the words "*The Parish of Appin, 1723*".

John McLauchlan accompanied the men from Appin who joined the 1745 Rising. He became chaplain-general to the clans and marched with them to Derby. He returned north with the army and was present at the battles of Falkirk and Culloden. The Appin chalice and paten were with him too - they are said to have been used at a Eucharist just before the Battle of Culloden. The chalice and paten were rescued from the battlefield along with the Stuart of Appin banner, perhaps even wrapped in the folds of the banner, and were eventually returned to Ballachulish, where they remain today in the Episcopal Church of Saint John.

As the remnants of the Jacobite army scattered, John McLauchlan did not return to Appin but travelled north, into hiding at Loch Broom in the highlands of Wester Ross. There he married Elizabeth Sutherland in 1748 and he ceased to be listed as incumbent of Appin around 1750.

There were other Episcopalian priests on Drummossie Moor at the Battle of Culloden. Both the Muster Roll of the Prince's army and the List of Prisoners of the Rising contain the names of several chaplains. Clan Cameron took its motto *Unite with Lochiel* seriously and was an ecumenical clan. Three chaplains are listed in the muster roll – the Reverend Duncan Cameron, of Fortingall (Episcopalian), the Reverend Alexander Cameron, brother of the Chief, (Roman Catholic) and the Reverend John Cameron, of Fort William (Presbyterian). Two present day retired bishops of the Scottish Episcopal Church - Bruce Cameron of Aberdeen and Orkney and Douglas Cameron of Argyll and the Isles - are currently honorary chieftains of Clan Cameron.

The saddest story of all the Scots priests of the 1745 Rising is that of the Reverend Robert Lyon. He was assistant priest in Perth and engaged to Stewart Rose, daughter of James Rose (Bishop of Fife 1731-33). When the Prince's army passed through Perth in September 1745, en route to Edinburgh and

Derby, the twenty year old David, Lord Ogilvy, offered his services. He raised the Forfarshire Regiment (Ogilvy's) and Robert Lyon joined immediately as chaplain.

At its maximum strength the regiment had 800 men and its uniform was a kilt or suit made in black and red check, the Rob Roy tartan. Robert Lyon stayed with the regiment, at his own expense, throughout the campaign. At Culloden Ogilvy's fought on the right wing of the second line. When the battle was lost they retreated in good order to Ruthven Barracks at Kingussie and a few days later to Clova in Angus, where the regiment was disbanded. Lord Ogilvy escaped to Norway and later served as a Lieutenant General in the French Army. He inherited the Earldom of Airlie in 1761, was pardoned by King George III in 1778, and returned to Scotland.

There was no pardon though for Robert Lyon. He was arrested, found guilty of high treason and of "levying war", although he had never carried a weapon of any sort.

The prison records show his gradual movement southward during the summer of 1746 - Montrose, Edinburgh, Carlisle and Penrith. In prison he celebrated the Eucharist for his fellow prisoners - the last recorded occasion being at Carlisle on October 15th 1746, when fifty people made their communion.

In a last letter, written to his mother and sisters on October 23rd 1746, he said *"And now my dear mother and sisters, it is my dying exhortation to you, as well as to every particular person who was committed to my spiritual care, steadfastly and constantly to continue in the faith and communion of our holy, persecuted mother, the Church of Scotland, of which I have the honour to die a very unworthy priest."*

Robert Lyon was hanged at Penrith on October 28th 1746, aged thirty-five - the Rising's one priestly martyr of the Scottish Episcopal Church.

The Chronological Story of the 18th Century

1701 King James VII and II dies and is succeeded by his son, who takes the title of King James VIII and III. He is recognised as the legitimate king by France, Spain and the Papal States as well as by many in the British Isles. *(*In this account the names of monarchs are given in the style in which they thought of themselves - irrespective of whether they were *de jure* or *de facto* rulers).

1701 In England the Act of Succession makes it impossible for a Roman Catholic to ascend the throne.

1702 King William dies and is succeeded by his sister-in-law, Anne - James VIII and III's second sister. She writes to the Scottish Privy Council saying that Episcopalians should be protected in the peaceful exercise of religion.

1704 The Archbishop of St Andrews and Primate of the Church, Arthur Rose, dies. His nephew, Alexander Rose, Bishop of Edinburgh, becomes also the Vicar-General of the Archdiocese of St Andrews. He is the first *Primus inter Pares* of the Church, the first among equals, but without the metropolitical authority exercised by Archbishops of St Andrews. (Primus still remains a unique title within Anglicanism today. Nearly all the churches of the Anglican Communion have Archbishops, although, instead, a few have a Presiding Bishop or Primate Bishop). Like almost all of the Scottish bishops during the next 150 years Alexander Rose is also the incumbent of a congregation, which provides his income.

1705 After the death of Archbishop Rose just five of the pre-Revolution bishops are left in office. During the fifteen years since the Revolution vacant dioceses have been left unfilled as the Jacobite bishops believe that it is the exiled king's right to issue the *congre d'elire*, the document authorising the appointment of bishops to specific dioceses. However, to ensure the Episcopal succession the bishops ordain some priests as bishops but without charge of dioceses. (By 1728 fourteen such bishops have been consecrated, eight of them during Alexander Rose's time as Primus).

1707 The Act of Succession is ratified by the Scottish Parliament and Sophia, Dowager Electress of Hanover and a grand-daughter of James VI and I, becomes heir apparent.

1707 The Union of the Parliaments of Scotland and England is implemented.

1708 James VIII and III attempts an invasion of Scotland. His French ships intend to land in the Firth of Forth but are intercepted by a Government fleet. The French admiral refuses to allow James to land, choosing retreat rather than the risk of battle.

1712 The fourth penal law - The Act of Toleration - requires Episcopalian clergy to pray for Queen Anne by name and also opens a route for Episcopalians willing to forsake allegiance to the exiled King James VIII. It is the beginning of the "Qualified" congregations – the last of which was reunited with the Episcopal Church in 1920. These congregations use the English Prayer Book and are ministered to by clergy who "qualify" under the Act of Toleration. The Act is further modified in 1746 and 1748.

1713 Under the Treaty of Utrecht, which ends the inconclusive Spanish War of Succession, one of the clauses concerns the expulsion of James VIII and III from France. It is two years before James moves to Rome, where he lives for the rest of his life.

1714 Sophia, Dowager Electress of Hanover and heir to the British throne, dies just two months before Queen Anne herself dies at the age of forty-nine. Sophia's son, and Anne's second cousin, George, Elector of Hanover, becomes King George I. There are more than fifty nearer claimants to the British throne than George but all, including James VIII and III, are Roman Catholics. The 1701 and 1707 Act of Succession debars them and George is the nearest non-Roman claimant.

1715 The Second Jacobite Rising begins. The Earl of Mar sails from London to Scotland and on September 6th raises the Standard of James VIII and III at Braemar amid 600 supporters. By October, Lord Mar's forces, nearly 20,000 now, control all Scotland north of the Forth, except Stirling Castle. However, a period of indecisiveness and inaction allows the Government forces to consolidate. In November the Jacobites march from Perth with the intention of taking Stirling. The Battle of Sherrifmuir on November 13th is inconclusive but on the same day Inverness surrenders to Government troops and a Jacobite force, led by John Mackintosh of Borlum, is defeated at Preston in England.

James VIII and III (known to the Hanoverians as the Old Pretender) is received on the quayside at Peterhead on December 22nd by William Dunbar, priest at Cruden Bay, but by the time the king meets Lord Mar at Fetteresso on January

9th 1716 the Jacobite army is less than 5,000. In contrast, the Duke of Argyll, Commander of the Government army, has acquired heavy artillery and is advancing steadily. Lord Mar orders the burning of villages between Perth and Stirling to deprive Lord Argyll's army of supplies. On January 30th the Jacobite army retreats northwards from Perth and on February 4th James writes a farewell letter to his supporters and sails from Montrose on February 5th. He is joined in exile by the Earl of Mar. Almost the entire Jacobite army is Episcopalian and, as a consequence, after the failure of the Rising, many clergy are removed from office by the Government, including thirty priests in the Diocese of Aberdeen.

1716 Two of the Scottish non-diocesan bishops - Archibald Campbell, who lives in England, and James Gadderar - meet with three English Non-Juring bishops in London, and Bishop Campbell speaks of private talks with Arsenius, Archbishop of Thebas, the representative of the Patriarch of Alexandria. There is hope of reunion with the Orthodox, but the negotiations eventually conclude without agreement.

1719 The third Jacobite Rising - England and France are at peace but Cardinal Giulio Alberoni encourages a Spanish invasion in support of James VIII and III. A storm scatters the twenty-seven ships of an invasion fleet before they can land 5000 soldiers in England. However, two ships bring a group of exiled Jacobites and 300 Spanish troops to Loch Duich. They briefly hold Eilean Donan Castle before a defeat at the Battle of Glen Shiel. Three of the Jacobite commanders (The Earl of Seaforth, Lord George Murray and Rob Roy McGregor) are wounded in the battle. A British force mounts a reprisal raid on the north-west coast of Spain, holding Vigo - from where the ships had sailed - for ten days before withdrawing. The Spanish prisoners are eventually returned to Spain.

1720 Bishop Rose of Edinburgh dies, the last remaining diocesan bishop in office. The Church now has four non-diocesan bishops living in Scotland and two living in London. Three of them take part in a meeting of the clergy of Edinburgh, a meeting which agrees both to fill the See and also that the clergy have a vote in the election. The senior bishop, by date of consecration, John Fullarton, a non-diocesan bishop since 1705, is not present but at a second meeting he is elected as Bishop of Edinburgh. The other bishops, under the title *The Episcopal College,* ratify the election and choose him as Primus. James Vlll is told of these events, gives his consent and writes to the Primus saying "The welfare of the Scots clergy I shall ever have at heart."

John Fullarton was born around 1645 and graduated from Glasgow University. He followed in his grandfather's steps by becoming incumbent of Kilmodan in Argyll. In 1684 he was appointed to the First Charge of Paisley Abbey, from which he was removed at the Revolution settlement of 1689. He was one of two priests who became the first non-diocesan bishops in 1705. A fervent Jacobite he was in regular contact with James Vlll's agent in Scotland, George Lockhart of Carnwath. Bishops are gradually appointed to some of the other dioceses and ultimately the system of both diocesan and non-diocesan bishops proves unsatisfactory as some of the bishops have oversight of specific districts while others do not. Disputes among the bishops continue regularly, particularly over the "Usages" – water added to the wine in the chalice at the Eucharist, the Epiclesis (a prayer asking for the coming of the Holy Spirit on the bread and wine), a prayer of Oblation and prayers for the dead.

1727 George I dies in Hanover, aged sixty-seven, and is succeeded by his son, George II.

1727 The Primus, John Fullarton dies, aged seventy-two, at his family estate, Greenhall at Kilmodan in Argyll, and is succeeded both as Bishop of Edinburgh and Primus by the seventy-eight year old Arthur Millar, a graduate of King's College, Aberdeen. He is the incumbent at Leith and has been a non-diocesan bishop since 1718. He dies after just five months as Primus, months of considerable difficulty for him as he faces hostility and non-co-operation from some of the bishops.

1727 Four diocesan bishops meet in Synod in Edinburgh and agree six Canons relating to the election of bishops and the appointment of deans.

1727 The clergy of Edinburgh diocese, without the approval of the bishops or James VIII, elect Andrew Lumsden as bishop. A graduate of Edinburgh University he followed his father and grandfather as incumbent of Duddingston until deposed in 1691 by the Commissioners of the Assembly for declining their authority. He became incumbent of the Barrenger's Close meeting house and Archdeacon of Edinburgh. He is consecrated by the Bishop of Brechin, the Co-Adjutor Bishop of Edinburgh and Bishop Andrew Cant, the only non-diocesan bishop willing to be present. Bishop Lumsden is appointed Primus.

1731 An Agreement is reached between the Scottish diocesan and non-diocesan bishops, which restores the concept of diocesan episcopacy (although the name *College of Bishops* and the role of *Primus* continues to this day). All the bishops agree to the six clauses of the Agreement, except that the Primus, Andrew Lumsden, dissents from the removal of possible metropolitan powers (which he has never used but thinks important to possess for the maintenance of dignity and order). The Agreement is significant in that it brings an end to any expectation of the involvement of the Crown – James VIII in exile or George II in London - in the governance of the Episcopal Church.

The meeting at which the Agreement is signed also brings to an end Andrew Lumsden's time as Primus. He is removed under Clause V of the Agreement just reached. He continues as Bishop of Edinburgh and as incumbent of Barrenger's Close until his death, aged sixty-nine, two years later.

The new Primus, at seventy-eight, is older. He is David Freebairn, a non-diocesan bishop since 1722 (his consecration having being requested by James VIII and III).

The 1731 Agreement also allocates areas of "inspection" to each of the bishops (similar to but not yet called dioceses) and Bishop Freebairn becomes Bishop of Galloway (along with Annandale, Nithsdale and Tweeddale) as well as Primus (the responsibilities of the office being to call the bishops together and preside at their meetings). All of this is combined with his continuing role as incumbent of the Baillie Fyfe's Close meeting house in Edinburgh. It is the first time that the Primus has not been the Bishop of Edinburgh – the previous understanding being that the order of seniority among the bishops was first the Archbishop of St Andrews (the last of whom died in 1704), secondly the Archbishop of Glasgow (the last died in 1708) and thirdly, by command of Charles II at the time of the creation of Edinburgh Diocese, the Bishop of Edinburgh.

1733 However, on the death of the former Primus, Andrew Lumsden, the present Primus, David Freebairn, succeeds him as Bishop of Edinburgh. He is an ardent Jacobite and a dispute arises over papers brought from France which the Primus wishes the other bishops to see. Most refuse to attend a meeting he calls and in 1735 there is another dispute over the consecration of Robert White as Bishop of Dunblane. The Primus and one other bishop oppose his nomination but three bishops consecrate him anyway.

1733 Arguments concerning the relationship between the Presbyterian Church of Scotland and the civil law in Scotland lead to a secession from the Church of Scotland. This First Secession arose over disputes over who had the power to nominate parish ministers. A Second Secession follows in 1761.

1738 The eighty-five year old David Freebairn is removed as Primus at a meeting of the bishops. Like his predecessor the deposed Primus continues his ministry as Bishop of Edinburgh and as incumbent of Baillie Fyfe's Close meeting house. He dies on Christmas Eve of the next year.

The new Primus, Thomas Rattray, is a member of a Jacobite family. He inherited the Craighall Estate at Rattray, Blairgowrie, Perthshire, in 1692 and, unlike his immediate predecessors and successors, he is not officially an incumbent of a congregation and is not dependent on such a position for his income. He lives at Craighall throughout his ministry. He was Bishop of Brechin from 1727 to 1731 and Bishop of Dunkeld from 1731. The most intellectual of the bishops, his interests include the enrichment of the Liturgy and the establishment of proper church order by means of a set of Canons.

1743 Thomas Rattray, the Primus, dies aged fifty-nine, before he sees much of his work come to fruition. He is succeeded as Primus by Robert Keith, Bishop of Caithness, Orkney and the Isles since 1731. (He was also Bishop of Fife from 1733 but resigned on being elected Primus). He is descended from the Keith family of Earls Marischal and had been educated at

Aberdeen Grammar School and Marischal College, Aberdeen. He was ordained deacon in 1710 and after three years as chaplain to the Earl of Erroll and the Dowager Countess in Cruden Bay, Aberdeenshire, he was ordained priest and began a ministry at Barrenger's Close meeting house in Edinburgh which lasted for the rest of his life.

1743 The meeting of bishops at which Robert Keith becomes Primus also agrees the Code of Canons, which had been written principally by Thomas Rattray. This is the first full attempt at revision since that - in the name of Charles I - in 1636. The new Canons provide the bedrock on which all future church legislation will be built.

1745 The fourth Jacobite Rising begins. It is led by the Prince Regent, Charles Edward Stuart, Bonnie Prince Charlie, (known to the Hanoverians as The Young Pretender). The Episcopal Church is less overtly involved than in the 1715 Rising, although the Prince's army is up to 70% Episcopalian and many of the Prince's Regiments have an Episcopalian chaplain. After initial successes, including the capture of Edinburgh, the Jacobite army marches into England. At Derby a Council of War decides to return to Scotland rather than continue the march on London.

In April 1746 the Prince's army is defeated at Culloden. At the time of the battle many of the Jacobite soldiers were tired and hungry. The previous night they had undertaken a fifteen mile night march to Nairn to attempt a surprise raid on the Duke of Cumberland's camp. However, the march took too long and it was daybreak before the raiders arrived. They returned to Culloden and awaited the coming of the the Government army. After the battle the Prince is hidden by supporters in the Highlands and Western Isles until his escape to France. In the aftermath of the Rising many Episcopal Churches are burned in the north and north-east. In some parts of

Scotland, particularly those which had sheltered the Bonnie Prince after Culloden, a revenge - verging on ethnic cleansing - is exacted.

The fifth penal law - The Toleration Act - requires all Episcopal priests to register their Letters of Orders and take Oaths of Allegiance to King George.

1748 The sixth penal law – The Penal Act - declares all previous registration of Orders to be void and Episcopal clergy are forbidden from conducting public worship. A priest is permitted to hold worship in a private house with not more than four people present, in addition to members of his family. Ingenious ways around the Act are devised – for example the service might be conducted from a central hallway with not more than four people in each of the rooms leading from it, with others listening outside the windows. In Peterhead the priest, Robert Kilgour, would on occasion lead fifteen such services a Sunday.

1751 John Wesley preaches in Musselburgh during the first of twenty-two visits to Scotland over thirty-nine years.

1757 The Primus, Robert Keith, dies, aged seventy-six, at his home in Donnington. Robert White, who had been Bishop of Dunblane from 1735 until 1743 and Bishop of Fife from 1743, is elected as Primus but continues also to be the incumbent at Cupar in Fife.

1760 George II dies and is succeeded by his son, George III. A relaxation of the rigorous enforcement of the penal laws gradually begins. Services are held more openly and some new churches built.

1761 The Primus, Robert White, dies and is succeeded in 1762 by William Falconer, Bishop of Moray since 1742. The new

Primus grew up in a wealthy family in Elgin and was educated at Oxford. He was ordained at the age of twenty-one and, after a seven year chaplaincy to the Laird of Balnagowan, became incumbent at Forres in Morayshire. He was incumbent in Elgin in 1741 when he was consecrated as Bishop Co-Adjutor to Robert Keith in Caithness and Orkney. He was elected Bishop of Moray in 1742. He resigned as incumbent of Elgin after the Battle of Culloden in 1746 and lived thereafter in Edinburgh.

1764 The Scottish Communion Office is published, the fruit of the work of Thomas Rattray two decades earlier and a collaboration between William Falconer and Robert Forbes, incumbent of Leith and Bishop of Ross, Caithness and Orkney since 1762. The Liturgy contains a long prayer of invocation of the Holy Spirit and has both Celtic and Eastern Orthodox influences. Its title page states, revealing the mind-set of the bishops, that it is "The Communion Office of the Church of Scotland".

1766 James VIII and III dies, having been king in exile for sixty-three years seven months and two days. He is buried at Saint Peter's in Rome and is succeeded by his son, Charles III, Bonnie Prince Charlie.

1776 The American Declaration of Independence is signed, the beginning of a long struggle for independence for the American colonies.

1776 William Falconer, the Primus, is elected as Bishop of Edinburgh, adding the responsibility to that of the Moray diocese (which he rarely visits since moving from Elgin and would resign two years later). His election ends a thirty-nine year long vacancy in Edinburgh diocese.

1782 The Primus, William Falconer, resigns, although remaining Bishop of Edinburgh. He is succeeded by Robert Kilgour, incumbent of Peterhead and Bishop of Aberdeen since 1768. He was born at Cruden Bay, Aberdeenshire, and graduated from King's College, Aberdeen. He was ordained in 1737 and immediately began his long ministry as incumbent of Peterhead, nine miles from his birthplace.

1783 The Treaty of Paris ends the American War of Independence and the United States becomes "a free, sovereign and independent nation". Oversight of the American Church by the Bishop of London is no longer appropriate and the clergy of Connecticut elect Samuel Seabury as bishop. He sails for London to seek consecration but English Law prevents it unless he takes an Oath of Allegiance to the Crown, which is an unacceptable condition.

1784 William Falconer, Bishop of Edinburgh and previously Primus, dies aged seventy-seven.

1784 Samuel Seabury comes to Scotland and is consecrated in Aberdeen as the first bishop for the United States by Robert Kilgour, Bishop of Aberdeen and Primus; Arthur Petrie, Bishop of Moray; and John Skinner, Co-Adjutor Bishop of Aberdeen. It is the beginning of a world-wide expansion of the Anglican Communion.

1786 Robert Kilgour resigns as Bishop of Aberdeen, to be succeeded by his Co-Adjutor, John Skinner. Bishop Kilgour continues as Primus for a further two years and as incumbent of Peterhead for a further three years – a total of fifty-three years of ministry in the Buchan town. He dies in March 1790, aged seventy-six.

1788 Charles III, Bonnie Prince Charlie, dies and is buried at Saint Peter's in Rome. He is succeeded by his brother, a Cardinal of the Roman Catholic Church, who becomes King Henry IX and I.

1788 Robert Kilgour resigns as Primus and is succeeded by John Skinner, son of the Dean of Aberdeen. He was ordained at the age of nineteen to serve the congregations in Ellon and Udny in Aberdeenshire. At the age of thirty he moved to Aberdeen, to a house in Longacre, the upper floor of which became a meeting house (the forerunner of Saint Andrew's Cathedral in Aberdeen). He became Co-Adjutor Bishop of Aberdeen in 1782, Bishop of Aberdeen in 1786 and Primus in 1788, aged forty-four.

1789 With the Stuart king a Cardinal, the Episcopal Church agrees to pray for King George III and three bishops (John Skinner of Aberdeen, John Strachan of Brechin and William Abernethy Drummond of Edinburgh) travel to London to petition for the repeal of the penal laws. A Bill passes in the House of Commons but fails in the House of Lords.

1792 At the second attempt the Scottish Episcopalians Relief Act is passed by both Houses of Parliament and the repression of the Church ends. However, the last hundred years have taken their toll - in 1689 there was a bishop for thirteen of the fourteen dioceses and six hundred clergy ministering to 66% of the population of Scotland. In 1792 there are four bishops and forty clergy ministering to 5% of the population. And, of course, the lifting of restrictions does not bring back the buildings lost in 1689. Under the careful leadership of the Primus, John Skinner, new churches begin to be built – a programme which accelerates throughout the nineteenth century, including the building of cathedrals in some dioceses and changing an existing church into a cathedral in others. The last Diocese to do so being Aberdeen and Orkney, where Saint Andrew's Church in King Street becomes the Cathedral for the Diocese in 1914.

Another Moment in the Century
True love ends in tears

A window in the Chancel of Barevan Church

The churchyard at Dunlichity, west of the Battlefield of Culloden, contains walled burial grounds for MacGillivray and Shaw clan chiefs. However, the grave of Alexander MacGillivray of Dunmaglass, who famously led Clan Chattan in a Highland charge at the Battle of Culloden, is not here but on

the shore of the Moray Firth at Petty. The story of his heroism is told at the battlefield and a stone marks the place where he died, just yards from the Government army's front line.
A memorial stone erected by Clan Macgillivray at the Old Churchyard of Petty tells the story of his death. The inscription says:

> ALEXANDER MACGILLIVRAY OF DUNMAGLASS ("ALASDAIR RUADH NA FEILE" -- GENEROUS RED-HEADED ALEXANDER),CHIEF OF HIS CLAN AND COLONEL OF THE MACKINTOSH OR CLAN CHATTAN REGIMENT, WAS BURIED ACROSS THE THRESHOLD OF A FORMER CHURCH ON THIS SITE. HE WAS MORTALLY WOUNDED BY A MUSKET SHOT WHILE LEADING THE HIGHLAND CHARGE AT THE BATTLE OF CULLODEN 16 APRIL 1746 AND DIED AT THE "WELL OF THE DEAD." HIS BODY WAS LATER RECOVERED AND INTERRED HERE.PLACED IN PROUD REMEMBRANCE BY THE CLAN MACGILLIVRAY. JULY 1997.

However, few people know the story of his romance. Not far from both Culloden and Petty, but on the other side of the River Nairn, trees on a bare hillside surround the remains of the 13th century Barevan Church. It was abandoned for a new church at Cawdor in 1619.

Long before Barevan was built another church stood here and was the burial place of the ancient rulers of the area, the Thanes of Cawdor. Their castle is close by and within it is kept a saint's bell, square sided and with a loop handle. It dates from the days of the Celtic church but, apart from the fact that it came from Barevan, no one now knows to whom it belonged.

What is known, though, is that where the Altar of Barevan church once stood a tombstone marks the grave of Elizabeth Campbell, the girl from Cawdor Castle whom Alexander MacGillivray loved. She died of a broken heart four months after Alexander's death at the Battle of Culloden. Fresh flowers are sometimes to be found on her grave, showing that the story of this love is not entirely forgotten.

Chapter 7
The 19th Century

In which the persecution is over. The Church becomes more democratic and its character is formed by the Oxford Movement.

A Moment in the Century
Persecution and an Argument are over

John Skinner, the Primus who
convened the meetings at Laurencekirk

What is usually known as the Synod of Laurencekirk is more properly described as a series of convocations. They were summoned by John Skinner, soon after he became Primus, and he made it clear at the first of the gatherings in

1789 that the meeting could not be called a Synod as there was no Canonical authority for a meeting which involved not just the bishops but also all the clergy and, for the first time ever, lay delegates from each congregation.

These were important meetings which sought to find ways out of two dilemmas. The Episcopal Church was still under the restrictions of the Penal Laws and an increasing number of people were opting to worship in the legal Qualified Chapels, which did not recognise the authority of the Episcopal Church.

The three meetings of the Convocation of Laurencekirk between 1789 and 1804 were ultimately successful in solving both problems, which had begun when the Penal Laws, imposed after the failure of the Jacobite Risings, started to bite hard. Some clergy were prepared to take the oath of allegiance to King George and, having been ordained by an English, Welsh or Irish bishop, were thus "qualified" to minister in (what became known as) "Qualified Congregations". Other clergy were either not willing to take the oath or, even if they were willing, had been ordained by a Scottish bishop, which meant that they could not do so. The 1748 Act said that any priest ordained by a Bishop of the Scottish Church could no longer have his Orders registered and could not conduct public worship, or even private prayers for his own family, if more than four people, other than family members, were present.

For many lay Episcopalians the appeal of the legal Qualified Chapels was obvious at a time when there were penalties for worshipping at an Episcopalian service. In some parts of the country the Qualified Chapels were strong while in others they failed completely. In Cruden Bay when Alexander Keith died in 1763, after nearly fifty years as schoolmaster and priest in Cruden, the Earl of Erroll built a Qualified Chapel but, rather than go there, the folks in Cruden walked the twelve miles to Ellon or the eight to Longside each Sunday depending on where the service was being held. In Ellon itself a Qualified Chapel lasted just four years.

But the split was there. The hope of a way out of the difficulties caused by the Penal Laws and the division in the Church came with the election of John Skinner as Coadjutor Bishop of Aberdeen in 1782.

The Bishop of Aberdeen and Primus, Robert Kilgour, was an old man now, but one who retained personal memories of when the bishops had deferred to the Stuart kings in exile. (There were three exiled kings whom the bishops recognised - James VII, who fled from London in 1688; James VIII, and Charles III, Bonnie Prince Charlie, and there was one whom they did not. He was Charles' younger brother, Henry I (Henry IX of England). He was perhaps the best of all the Stuarts but - at least in the eyes of the Scottish bishops - he had the disadvantage of being a Cardinal bishop of the Roman Catholic Church).

So, at the death of Charles III in 1788, Bishop Kilgour accepted that it was the end of the road for the Stuart kings in Scotland and resigned as Primus, having given up the See of Aberdeen two years earlier. The way was clear for those who wished to make a new beginning.

When John Skinner became Primus in 1788 he immediately began to work for a settlement of the two problems which beset the Church. At an Episcopal Synod in Aberdeen on April 24th 1788 the bishops agreed that as from May 25th that year prayers would be said for King George III and the Royal Family. The first Convocation of Laurencekirk in 1789 deputed Bishops Skinner, Abernethy-Drummond and Strachan to travel to

London to ask for a repeal of the Penal Laws. The first attempt passed in the House of Commons but not in the House of Lords. A three year campaign in Scotland and London led to the passing of the Relief Act on June 15th 1792. The Penal Laws were, essentially, gone - although a few remnants of them lingered for longer.

There was still, however, the question of the Qualified congregations. They were ministered to by priests, many of whom were Scots who had been ordained by English, Welsh or Irish bishops. They were not, however, subject to the authority of any of these bishops and, especially, they did not recognise the authority of the Scottish bishops. At the maximum there were twenty-nine Qualified congregations, and by the time the Penal Laws were repealed twenty-four of them remained. Bishop Skinner had early successes in persuading some of the Qualified congregations in Aberdeen diocese to unite with the Episcopal Church - Banff in 1792 and Cruden in 1801 were the first, and priests from both places were at the Convocation of Laurencekirk in 1804, at which the principal business was acceptance of the Thirty-Nine Articles of Religion as a public Confession of Faith. The acceptance brought the Scottish Church into line with both the Qualified Congregations and the Church of England.

Who made the decision in 1804? John Skinner, obviously, and three other bishops. They were Andrew Macfarlane of Ross, Jonathan Watson of Dunkeld, and Alexander Jolly of Moray. Two bishops were not present – John Strachan of Brechin, who was too infirm to come and William Abernethy-Drummond of Edinburgh, for whose absence no explanation is known. There were also thirty-eight priests and two deacons present as well as lay delegates - a total of eighty-four people in all. Nearly all the clergy of the Church came, excepting those who were too ill or too old to travel.

Why at Laurencekirk? It was a convenient place. Most of the clergy lived north of the Tay, and Laurencekirk, amid the rolling countryside of the Mearns, provided a good meeting place, with, from 1792, the added advantage of having a bishop living in the village. At that time it was normal for bishops also to be parish priests and in Laurencekirk the incumbent from 1791 was Jonathan Watson, who became Bishop of Dunkeld in 1792.

How he came to be in Laurencekirk is in itself quite a story. Laurencekirk had grown from a tiny hamlet to a substantial village in the years that Lord Gardenston, a judge in Edinburgh, had been the laird. He was a Presbyterian but he was very pleased to hear that the first Convocation of Laurencekirk in 1789 was to be held in his village. He asked the Presbyterian Minister for help in accommodating those who would come. The Minister declined, saying that he had little time for Episcopalians. The Laird then told him that if that was the case the Minister would be seeing much more of them. The Laird said he would build and endow a church and also a house for the priest - and he did.

Bishop Skinner achieved what he set out to do at the Laurencekirk meetings. The Penal Laws were repealed and there was no longer a need for the Qualified Chapels to exist separately from the Episcopal Church. Less than a month after the Laurencekirk meeting in 1804 Daniel Sandford, incumbent of the Charlotte Street Qualified Chapel in Edinburgh brought his large congregation into the Episcopal Church and, a sign that the rift was over, was elected as Bishop of Edinburgh in 1806. However, it took until 1920 until the last of the Qualified Chapels - at Montrose - came in.

The Chronological Story of the 19th Century

1804 Under the leadership of the Primus, John Skinner, the Convocation of Laurencekirk begins a process which brings together the former "Non-Juring" and "Qualified" strands of the Church. (At the time of the meeting there were twenty Qualified congregations and by 1813 thirteen of them had become part of the Episcopal Church. The process continued until 1920 when the last of the Qualified Chapels joined the Episcopal Church).

The Thirty-nine Articles of Religion are also accepted at the Laurencekirk Synod, beginning a rapprochement with the Church of England, a process which culminated in 1864 when the last barrier is removed, allowing priests ordained by Scottish bishops to hold office within the Church of England.

1807 King Henry IX and I dies and becomes the third Stuart king in exile to be buried in Saint Peter's in Rome. He had been a Cardinal of the Roman Catholic Church for sixty years. Under the terms of his Will (which he signs with the royal initial R (for Rex) after his name) he leaves the crown jewels which James VII and II had taken with him into exile in France to the future King George IV and names his own successor in his claim to the throne as his cousin and nearest relative, Charles Emmanuel IV, former King of Sardinia.

Following the death of his wife, Charles Emmanuel abdicated as King of Sardinia in favour of his brother Victor Emmanuel, although retaining the personal title of king, and lived in Rome and Frascati. He made no public claim to the British Crown and in 1815, at the age of sixty-four, took simple vows in the Society of Jesus and lived the rest of his life in the Jesuit novitiate in Rome.

1809 The Synod of Bishops meets in Aberdeen and agrees six Canons.

1810 A Theological College for the Episcopal Church is founded.

Miss Kathein Panton of Fraserburgh, a member of the saintly Bishop Alexander Jolly's congregation in Fraserburgh, endowed the College and appointed Fraserburgh born James Walker as Pantonian Professor (a title still in use in today's Theological Institute). He held the appointment until his death in 1841. He was also Bishop of Edinburgh from 1830 and Primus from 1837. The College had no students in its first years and, when some appeared, James Walker taught them in his own home. His successor as Pantonian Professor and Bishop of Edinburgh was Charles Terrot. He was also Primus from 1857 to 1862. He taught his students at 8 Hill Street, Edinburgh, and then in Saint Andrew's Hall in the High Street.

When Trinity College, Glenalmond, opened in 1847 the College transferred to Perthshire and became the Senior Department of Glenalmond. Bishop Terrot remained Pantonian Professor unil 1863. He resigned as Primus in 1862 and died, still Bishop of Edinburgh, in 1872. Four years later the bishops decided that training should again be centred in Edinburgh, although for the next four years the College had no fixed home. In 1880 a house at 9 Rosebery Crescent was rented and in 1891 Coates Hall purchased. The College was replaced by the dispersed Theological Institute of the Scottish Episcopal Church in 1994 and Coates Hall is now home to Saint Mary's Music School and the Choir School of Saint Mary's Cathedral, Edinburgh.

1811 A General Synod meets with two Houses – one of bishops and the other of deans and representative clergy. The principal business is the revision of the 1743 and 1809 Canons, which had been agreed by the bishops alone. The Scottish Communion Office becomes the primary authorised Liturgy and the English one (used in the Qualified Chapels) secondary but permitted. There is also a recommendation that the surplice replace the black gown as appropriate wear for clergy at services because white is "the proper sacerdotal vestment" used by both the Jewish and Christian priests and "seems to be a much more appropriate dress for ministers of the Prince of Peace than black". There are twenty-six Canons in the 1811 Code.

1814 Hanover becomes a kingdom in its own right and George III becomes also King of Hanover.

1816 John Skinner, the Primus and Bishop of Aberdeen, dies in office, aged seventy-two. He had been a bishop in Aberdeen for thirty-four years and Primus for twenty-eight. He is succeeded as Primus by George Gleig, incumbent of Stirling since 1797, Co-Adjutor Bishop of Brechin from 1808 to 1810 and Bishop of Brechin since 1810. He makes a visitation to the Brechin diocese every three years (but in his final ten years is not able to go at all). He is a prolific writer and an editor of the *Encyclopaedia Britannica*.

1820 Matthew Luscombe, a priest in Paris, is consecrated as a bishop by the Primus, George Gleig, and two other Scottish bishops, to serve British Anglicans living in France. Following the consecration of Samuel Seabury, as the first bishop in the United States thirty-four years earlier, it is a further step in the establishment of a worldwide Anglican Communion.

1820 George III dies and is succeeded by his son, George IV. He has already ruled as Prince Regent during the nine years of his father's illness.

1828 and 1829 A General Synod meets at Laurencekirk and agrees changes to the Code of Canons – a new title page names the Church as *The Protestant Episcopal Church in Scotland*. The word "Protestant" is removed ten years later.

1829 The Parliament at Westminster passes the Roman Catholic Relief Act, which removes the penal laws applied to Roman Catholics.

1833 The Oxford Movement begins in England with the aim of restoring the High Church ideals of the seventeenth century. It appeals to many in Scotland as the Episcopal Church holds a high view of sacramental doctrine, although its practice has been ascetic and simple. There is now a gradual introduction of greater ritual, reflected in both worship and the architecture of new church buildings.

1830 George IV dies and is succeeded by his younger brother, William IV.

1830 Episcopal vacancies provide an opportunity to re-organise dioceses. Glasgow and Galloway is separated from Edinburgh to form a new diocese; Moray is joined with Ross and Fife added to Dunkeld and Dunblane (it is eventually called the Diocese of St Andrews, Dunkeld and Dunblane).

1837 George Gleig resigns as Primus, aged eighty-three, after twenty-one years in the role. He continues as incumbent of Stirling and Bishop of Brechin. The new Primus is John Walker. He was born in Fraserburgh, Aberdeenshire, and had been Bishop of Edinburgh since 1830, having resigned as incumbent of Saint Peter's, Edinburgh, on his consecration. A diligent bishop he visits all the congregations in the diocese.

1837 William IV dies and is succeeded as monarch by his niece, Victoria. However, the direct link between the British and Hanoverian thrones ends as succession laws in Hanover preclude a woman from the throne. Victoria's uncle, the Duke of Cumberland and Teviotdale, became King of Hanover. (The final king, George V of Hanover, was deposed in 1866 when the kingdom was annexed by Prussia. He died in 1878 and was buried in Saint George's Chapel, Windsor).

1838 A General Synod meets and revises the Code of Canons – the word "Protestant" is removed from the title page; formal recognition of the role of co-adjutor bishops is given; the surplice replaces the black gown as the mandatory and "proper sacerdotal vestment" and the Scottish Episcopal Church Society is founded to provide a fund for aged and infirm clergy, grants for congregations in difficulty, assistance for ordinands and Episcopalian school teachers and for the creation of diocesan libraries.

1840 The former Primus, George Gleig, dies in Stirling, where he had been incumbent for forty-three years. He had been Co-Adjutor and then Bishop of Brechin for twenty-nine years.

1840 A Bill is passed by both Houses of Parliament which removes a restriction on any priest ordained by a Scottish bishop from officiating in English parish churches.

1841 The Primus, John Walker, dies in Edinburgh, aged seventy. He has been Bishop of Edinburgh for eleven years and Primus for four. His successor as Primus is William Skinner, Bishop of Aberdeen since 1816 and son of the former Primus, John Skinner. William Skinner is a graduate of both Marischal College, Aberdeen and Wadham College, Oxford. Like many others in this period, in order to avoid the remaining penalty of the penal laws, he sought ordination outwith Scotland. He was ordained by the Bishop of St Asaph in 1802 and served as his father's assistant in Saint Andrew's Chapel, which had been built next to the original meeting house in Longacre, Aberdeen. He succeeded his father, both as incumbent and as Bishop of Aberdeen, in 1816. The following year the Longacre congregation moved to a new church in King Street (which is now Saint Andrew's Cathedral).

1842-1880 In a reaction against the Oxford Movement some congregations leave the Episcopal Church, objecting to a change in the Canons which seeks to prevent non-liturgical services. They describe themselves as "English Episcopal Chapels". Eventually the number of congregations, including several private chapels, is twenty-four. They regard themselves as under the authority of the Church of England, although the Church of England does not so regard them. All their clergy have been ordained by English, Welsh or Irish bishops. Samuel Gobat, Bishop in Jerusalem, and Edmund Beckles, retired Bishop of Sierra Leone, oversee the English Episcopal Chapels at different times. In the late 19th and 20th centuries these congregations gradually re-enter the Episcopal Church, the last to do so being Saint Silas', Glasgow, in 1986.

1843 The unease in the Church of Scotland over who appoints ministers, and the Church's relationship to the State, leads to The Disruption in which 450 ministers and thousands of lay people leave the Church of Scotland to form the Free Church of Scotland. The various seceding groups proliferate to form more Presbyterian denominations.

1847 The election of Alexander Penrose Forbes as Bishop of Brechin in 1847, at the age of thirty, gives added impetus to the emerging Oxford Movement in Scotland. The new bishop had come under its influence while a student at Oxford. Further up the Tay, Saint Ninian's Cathedral in Perth originates as a Mission Church in the Oxford Movement tradition in 1846 and work on the Cathedral begins soon afterwards. Its foundation stone is the first for a cathedral to be laid in Scotland since that at Fortrose Cathedral in the 14th century.

Also in 1847 Trinity College, Glenalmond, is another fruit of the Oxford Movement. It is founded by William Gladstone and James Robert Hope as a place where young men can be trained for the ministry of the Episcopal Church and where the sons of the laity can be educated and brought up in the faith and tradition of the Church. (The school continues today as Glenalmond College, a boarding and day school for boys and girls aged between twelve and eighteen)

1849 The influence of the Oxford Movement continues and the College of the Holy Spirit is built by the Earl of Glasgow on the Isle of Cumbrae "for the frequent Celebration of Divine Service by a Collegiate Body under circumstances favourable to religious learning". The Earl envisages five Canons and seven Choristers being resident. The College church becomes the Cathedral of the Isles, within the Diocese of Argyll and the Isles, in 1876.

Between 1849 and 1885 the College operated as a theological college and, for two years following the Second World War, served as Cumbrae Test School, at which ex-service candidates for ordination received preliminary training. Both Cathedral and College continue today, with the College in use as a residential retreat centre.

1850 The Episcopal training Institution is founded to train men as teachers in Episcopalian day schools and is followed, in 1855, by the School Mistresses' Training School. In 1920 the secular part of the training of teachers became the responsibility of the National Committee for the Training of

Teachers and in 1928 the training of all Episcopalian teachers transferred to (what was to become) Moray House School of Education in the University of Edinburgh. The Episcopalian College, Dalry House, continued to provide two hours of training each week in religious education and also served as a hostel for students. It closed in 1934.

1857 The Primus, William Skinner dies, aged seventy-nine. He has been Primus for sixteen years and Bishop of Aberdeen for forty-one. He is succeeded by Charles Terrot, Bishop of Edinburgh since 1841 and the first Englishman to be elected as Primus. He had been born in Cuddalore in South India (where his father was an officer in the army of the East India Company). He was educated at Carlisle Grammar School and Trinity College, Cambridge, and was ordained in Bristol in 1813. However, during the next year he succeeded his uncle as priest of the Qualified Chapel at Haddington in East Lothian, which in the following year became part of the Episcopal Church. In 1816 he moved to Edinburgh – first to Saint Peter's and then in 1833 to Saint Paul's, York Place. He remained incumbent there for the rest of his life. He became Dean of Edinburgh in 1837 and Pantonian Professor and Bishop of Edinburgh in 1841. During the following years the diocese saw new churches built and the appointment of a diocesan missionary with the specific task of seeking the poor and linking them into the life of local churches.

1857 The Bishop of Brechin, Alexander Penrose Forbes, delivers a Charge to his Diocesan Synod in which he stresses the real presence of Christ in the Eucharist. The other Bishops send a pastoral letter to the Church, to be read at each Diocesan Synod, disagreeing with Bishop Forbes. Formal proceedings in the Episcopal Synod lead to the censure and admonition of Bishop Forbes. (A century later what he said would be the view of much, but not all, of the Episcopal Church).

1862 Charles Terrot resigns as Primus, aged seventy-four, after a stroke. He remains Bishop of Edinburgh, with a co-adjutor appointed.

He is succeeded as Primus by Robert Eden, aged fifty-eight. He has been Bishop of Moray and Ross since 1851. The son of an English baronet he was educated at Westminster School and Christ Church, Oxford. He was ordained in 1827 and after three curacies became Rector of Leigh-on Sea in Essex. Following his election as Bishop of Moray and Ross he became incumbent at Elgin, with just seven other clergy in the diocese.

1862 A Sister from the Society of Saint Margaret comes to Aberdeen from the Mother House in East Grinstead to undertake parish work – the first member of a religious order to work within the Episcopal Church. Within two years Saint Margaret's Scottish house was established and later acquired independent status, with its own Mother Superior and novitiate. The Sisters ran homes for children and for the aged in buildings adjacent to the Convent in the Spital, (where they moved in 1874) and also a guest house within the Convent itself. At various times Sisters worked in Lerwick, Oban, Fraserburgh and Dundee. Following the death of Mother Verity in 2002 the two remaining Sisters became part of the Saint Margaret Community at Walsingham, in Norfolk, although one of the two, Sister Columba, continues to live and work in Aberdeen.

The 2012-2013 Year Book of the Scottish Episcopal Church lists three women's communities as being active within the Episcopal Church – The Franciscan Hermits of the Transfiguration at Loanhead, near Edinburgh (founded in 1965 as an ecumenical community with a Cistercian rule); the Society of Our Lady of the Isles on the Isle of Fetlar in Shetland (founded in 1988 with a rule which is a blend of Celtic, Franciscan and Carthusian) and the Carmel Community on the Isle of Lewis.

Other women's communities founded in Scotland but no longer in existence are -
·   The Community of Saint Andrew of Scotland in Edinburgh (1867).
·   The Community of Saint Mary and Saint John in Perth (1870) and transferred to Aberdeen and Ellon (1873). The Community closed in 1980.
·   The Sisterhood of Saints Mary and Modwenna in Dundee (1871). The Community closed in 1988.
·   The Order of Holy Charity in Edinburgh (1872) out of which grew the Order of the Holy Comforter (1891).

Some English Communities also established Houses in Scotland, although, none now continues in Scotland.
·   The Society of All Saints began work in Edinburgh in 1870
·   The Community of the Epiphany worked at Saint Ninian's Cathedral, Perth, from 1905 to 1923.
·   The Society of Saint Peter the Apostle, Horbury, Yorkshire, took over the running of the Saint Andrew's Home for Girls in Edinburgh in 1919 from the Community of Saint Andrew of Scotland. In 1930 the Saint Peter's Community divided into two independent Houses and four groups of Sisters from one of them, the Community of Saint Peter the Apostle, Westminster, worked in Scotland at Saint Andrew's Home, Edinburgh; All Saints' Mission House, Edinburgh; and retreat houses at Balhousie Castle, near Perth, and Sunnybrae at Walkerburn in the Borders, the last to survive. The Sisters withdrew from Walkerburn in 1976.

- The Order of the Holy Paraclete, based in Whitby in Yorkshire, sent Sisters to assist in staffing Scottish Churches' House in Dunblane in the 1980s and 1990s and also worked in Mid-Craigie, Dundee, from 1996-1999. The Order has its mother house in Whitby and its five branch houses in Britain are currently all in Yorkshire.

Fewer communities of men have worked in Scotland and only one appears in the 2012-2013 Year Book –
- The Franciscan Hermits of the Transfiguration at Roslin, near Edinburgh, founded in 1965 and - like the women's community at Loanhead – it is ecumenical and has a Cistercian rule.

In the past other groups have also worked in Scotland –
- Monks from the Society of Saint John the Evangelist (the Cowley Fathers) were at Bishop's House on the Isle of Iona from 1897 to 1909. Members of the Society returned to Scotland in 1942 and lived at Doune in Perthshire. One of the priests was Rector of Saint Modoc's Church and Superior of the Community living in The Rectory. In 1946 the Society left Doune and lived at Saint John's Mission House in Joppa until withdrawing from Scotland in 1954.
- Brothers of the Society of Saint Francis worked in both Glasgow and in Edinburgh for some years from 1978 and in Dundee from 2003 to 2005.

1863 The Primus, Robert Eden, presides at a General Synod which agrees a complete revision of the Code of Canons. Lay Electors are allowed a role for the first time in choosing bishops, the formal beginning of lay involvement in the government of the Church. (When Bishop Eden had been elected bishop twelve years earlier the electorate consisted simply of the seven priests in the Moray and Ross diocese - five voted for his election and two did not).

1864 With the removal of, effectively, the last piece of the penal laws, priests ordained by Scottish bishops can hold office within the Church of England.

1864 The Diocese of Caithness is added to Moray and Ross and the Primus, Robert Eden, now becomes Bishop of Moray, Ross and Caithness.

1865 The ministry of Lay Reader is established in the Scottish Episcopal Church.

1866 The foundation stone of a Saint Andrew's Cathedral in Inverness is laid by the Archbishop of Canterbury, Charles Longley – a public recognition of the Episcopal Church by the Church of England.

1871 Requests for the Episcopal Church to take financial responsibility for mission work in Kaffaria in South Africa and the Mission District of Chandra in India are accepted, and the first bishop for the Diocese of St John's, Transkei, South Africa, is consecrated in Edinburgh in 1873. Over subsequent years priests from Scotland serve in both areas and the link with the Diocese of Mthatha (as St John's has been called since 2006) continues – it is one of Aberdeen and Orkney's partner dioceses, the other being Connecticut, a link stretching back to the consecration of Samuel Seabury in 1784.

1871 The Irish Church Act (passed by the Westminster Parliament in 1869) comes into effect and the Church of Ireland is dis-established, that is, separated from the State and the requirement that tithes be paid to it removed. Irish bishops cease to be members of the House of Lords.

1872 The former Primus, Charles Terrot, dies aged eighty-two. He has been Bishop of Edinburgh for thirty-one years.

1875 Alexander Penrose Forbes, Bishop of Brechin for twenty-eight years, dies aged fifty-eight. Although never chosen as Primus, he laid the foundations for the development of the Episcopal Church from the mid-19th century onwards. In Brechin diocese he oversaw the building of churches and schools and also played a role in many areas of life in and around Dundee.

1875 The Aberlour Orphanage is founded by Canon Charles Jupp in the Speyside village of Aberlour. At first Canon and Mrs Jupp cared for just four "mitherless bairns" in one cottage. The Canon remained priest of Saint Margaret's, Aberlour, and Warden of the Orphanage until his death in 1911, never wavering from his view that every child has the ability and right to flourish. At its peak, following the First World War, five hundred children were in care. The Orphanage closed in 1967 and the Aberlour Child Care Trust continues its work of caring for Scotland's children today.

1876 Further revision of the Code of Canons takes place at a General Synod in Edinburgh. Among the provisions is the establishing of The Representative Church Council, giving laity a voice, along with bishops and clergy, in the governance of the church's finances and administration. It remains the Church's administrative body until the creation of the present General Synod structure in 1982. There are forty-seven Canons in the 1876 Code.

1878 Pope Leo XIII restores the Scottish hierarchy of the Roman Catholic Church. Bishops are appointed to cover some of the ancient dioceses with new dioceses of Motherwell and Paisley being created. During the years of persecution a hidden network of priests had ministered in Scotland but only in a few areas, such as the Western Isles and some Highland glens, were Roman Catholics a significant percentage of the population. This changed with 19th century immigration from Ireland into the west of Scotland and this, together with freedom from persecution and growing confidence, contributed to the Pope's decision – eighteen years after a similar restoration in England.

1886 The increasingly frail Robert Eden resigns after twenty-four years as Primus. He becomes priest of the Chapel of the Holy Spirit (now Saint Michael and All Angels) in Inverness, a church founded in 1877 to minister to the poor of the town. Bishop Eden dies in 1888.

The new Primus is Hugh Willoughby Jermyn, Bishop of Brechin since 1876 and previously Bishop of Colombo in (what is now) Sri Lanka. He was born in Cambridgeshire and educated at Westminster School and Trinity Hall, Cambridge University. Bishop Jermyn has a history of over-working (he had breakdowns in health in the West Indies as Archdeacon of St Christopher's and also later as Bishop of Colombo - he returned to Britain after four years in the diocese. However, during his twenty-seven years as Bishop of Brechin the first twenty are fruitful as he builds on the foundations laid by his predecessor in Brechin, Alexander Penrose Forbes - new churches open and the number of communicants almost doubles.

1888 The bishops of the Anglican Communion at the Lambeth Conference (in a document known as *The Lambeth Quadilateral* define four areas deemed essential for a united church - the Bible as the ultimate standard of faith; the Apostle's and Nicene Creeds as statements of faith; the sacraments of Baptism and the Eucharist; and the historic

Episcopate. However, the only churches with which the Episcopal Church is in communion are all Anglican but as the 20th century progresses non-Anglican churches are added – the Old Catholic Churches of Europe, the Philippines Independent Church, the Lusitanian Church of Portugal, the Spanish Reformed Church and the Mar Thoma Church of Kerala in south-west India. The Churches of North India, Pakistan, Bangladesh and South India are considered special cases as all were formed - at various times after British rule ended in the Indian sub-continent in 1948 - by a union of the Anglican Church with other denominations. All are now provinces of the Anglican Comunion. In the second half of the 20th century the Lutheran Churches in Scandinavia, Germany and France are added.

1890 At a General Synod there are further changes to the Code of Canons. "Rector" replaces "Incumbent" as the ordinary title of a priest in charge of a congregation and it is agreed that the Representative Church Council will not deal with questions of doctrine, worship or discipline, these being the concern of the newly named Provincial Synod. A proposal that the Primus be known as Archbishop is rejected (although the Primus will now be styled "The Most Reverend").

1891 The Theological College moves to Coates Hall in Edinburgh (it remains there until a dispersed Institute replaces it in 1994).

1894 The Bishop of Argyll and the Isles, Alexander Chinnery-Haldane, founds Saint Columba's House, on the Isle of Iona, as a centre of Prayer, Study and Eucharist (the house, now known as Bishop's House, continues this role as a residential retreat centre).

1896 Pope Leo XIII in a Papal Bull *Apostolicae Curae* declares Anglican Orders to be null and void.

Another Moment in the Century
Parson Duncan - a faithful priest

the Reverend Duncan Mackenzie

Duncan Mackenzie was born in Ballachulish around 1783 and spent most of his adult life ministering to the people of the Diocese of Moray and Ross, of which he became Archdeacon, and more particularly to the people of Strathnairn, where he lived.

Most people in Scotland today struggle to place Strathnairn - it's a wild, lonely glen in the mountains on the south side of Loch Ness. At the Revolution of 1690 the majority of the people were Episcopalians and it was not until the large scale emigration of the 19th century that the Episcopalian population thinned at all.

The easiest way to find Strathnairn is from the A9 road between Aviemore and Inverness. Five miles south of Inverness the B851, signposted for Fort Augustus, leads off to the west. The road follows the course of the River Nairn through woods and hills and the settlements of Inverarnie, Farr, Flichity, Brin and Croachy. In the latter is the present day Episcopal Church of Saint Paul, which was built on the site of Duncan Mackenzie's church in 1868. The road goes on through Aberarder and Dunmaglass and over the hill into Stratherrick, with its villages of Errogie, Gorthleck and Whitebridge, before coming to Fort Augustus at the head of Loch Ness.

Duncan Mackenzie trained for the ministry with the Reverend John Murdoch, the priest in Keith, spending the winters studying at King's College, Aberdeen, from where he graduated with a Master of Arts degree in 1817. At King's he also took a more formal interest in Gaelic, his native language, and was later, during his Strathnairn years, to translate Scriptures and the Prayer Book into Gaelic. He also did some medical studies and this was to serve the people of Strathnairn well.

He was ordained deacon in the year of his graduation and appointed incumbent of Strathnairn. He was ordained priest two years later and immediately was given added responsibility as incumbent of Dingwall, thirty miles away. He remained in Strathnairn until his death 41 years later, although he resigned the charge at Dingwall after 32 years. During those years he was in Strathnairn and Dingwall on alternate Sundays. He also spent eight years as priest of Fortrose (1832-1840) and, for the five years before his death

(1853-1858), was also priest of the Gaelic Mission in Inverness. In addition to all of this, as Archdeacon of Moray and Ross, he travelled throughout the north, both on foot and on horseback. His silver plated stirrups are preserved at Saint Paul's.

Parson Duncan was prepared to minister to everyone, without thought of denomination, and was greatly liked and valued for his care, love and generosity. The medical skills he had acquired were as appreciated, and as freely given, as the spiritual ones.

In Strathnairn services were initially held in a church at Knocknacroshaig, near Brin Rock. The church was built in 1817, the year Duncan Mackenzie came to the glen. It is thought that it was destroyed in a fire and thereafter he held services in the open, while building another church at Croachy. He built this church with his own hands and he and Florence, his wife, lived in two rooms adjoining it.

In later years his generosity to those in need could no longer be funded from his stipend of £15 a year and so, to augment it, he took on the tenancy of a farm at Tullich, looking over Loch Ruthven. He died, still ministering and farming, aged seventy-five, in 1858 and is buried back home in Argyll, in the churchyard of Saint John's at Ballachulish. His wife outlived him by seven years.

The present Saint Paul's was built on the site of Parson Duncan's church at Croachy in 1868 and the west wall contains a rose window memorial to this great priest. One of his family members is a priest in today's Episcopal Church - the Very Reverend Norman MacCallum, former Provost of Oban Cathedral.

Saint Paul's Church and Hall in Strathnairn - built on the site of Parson Duncan's church

Chapter 8
The 20th Century

In which new churches open and modern language Liturgy is introduced. There is a greater focus on Ecumenism and Mission. And the ordination of women begins.

A Moment in the Century
Two Country Churches - their story

Saint James's at Cruden Bay and Saint Mary-on-the-Rock at Ellon

Gerald Stranraer-Mull writes:

I went to Saint Mary-on-the-Rock at Ellon and Saint James at Cruden Bay as Rector in 1972, and stayed until retirement thirty-six years later. Both churches are at the heart of communities in rural Buchan in Aberdeenshire, and, forty years ago, each had small congregations. They were far away places - the Diocesan magazine in 1896 describing how to get there said that it was necessary to go *Aff the earth and doon tae Buchan*. But in the 1970s, with the discovery of off-shore oil and gas, the population of these welcoming places grew, and with the growth came many newcomers to church.

The first lesson we learned was not to do the usual Episcopalian thing and wait for months before asking anyone new to be fully involved in the life of the Church. People were just not in Aberdeenshire for that long. Many of the people were gifts from God, some for the longer haul and others for a much shorter time. One of the short term people was a young woman with the amazing ability to bring children to church. Within weeks of her arrival all the children in her street were coming to (what was at the time called) Saint Mary's Sunday School, soon to be followed by kids from the neighbouring streets, and there were eighty children around each Sunday. The same thing happened in Cruden Bay, with a Sunday School gathering in the village primary school, and in Collieston where an ecumenical children's group began to meet. Other young women, but with a gift for music this time, encouraged people to sing or play music - the choir in Ellon grew to around thirty, and had a small orchestra in addition.

We also owed much to visitors who came to us from outwith Ellon and Cruden Bay. They were people that I could not have expected to find in small country congregations which were after all "aff the earth" - Terry Fullam, Rector of Saint Paul's, Darien, the fastest growing Episcopal Church in the United States; Noel Tredinnick, founder and conductor of the All Souls' Orchestra from London (with some of the orchestra); Alastair Haggart, Ted Luscombe and Richard Holloway during each's time as Primus; other bishops from Scotland, Australia, France, New Zealand, Norway, Papua New Guinea, Singapore, South Africa, Tanzania, the United States and Zambia; and the Secretary-General of the Anglican Communion. They, along with successive Bishops of Aberdeen and Orkney and many others, gave us encouragement and nourishment.

The Churches became pretty full every Sunday (forty years ago the regular Sunday attendance at Cruden Bay was under ten and in Ellon under twenty but the number rose to fifty in Cruden Bay and a hundred and fifty in Ellon). Mid-week attendance also increased, particularly the Wednesday morning Eucharist in Ellon, which now included music, hymns and a sermon. There were often thirty people there and sometimes many more.

A hall was built at Saint Mary's (and has since been twice extended) and Saint James's was repaired, re-designed internally and refurbished. A crucial part of all this building work was the creation of large carparks in fields adjacent to both churches, a particularly expensive project in Ellon - the church is very accurately called Saint Mary-on-the-Rock - as it was clear that most people drove to the churches and the original parking was limited. To pay for it all the finances of both congregations were put on a sound footing through careful and thoughtful stewardship campaigns, which put the needs of church and community to the congregations' members, inviting their response in money or involvement or both.

Eventually the short-term people who had been such a gift moved on leaving us with a wonderful legacy - the confidence to reach out to the whole community and not just to those who thought of themselves as church people or Episcopalians. One immediate result was that the notice boards were changed, taking out the word "Episcopal" - a word puzzling to some and a barrier to others. The boards now just gave the name of the church and the words *A Church for Everyone*. Very soon the congregations included people whose ecclesiastical origin had been in the Baptist, Brethren, Lutheran, Methodist, Presbyterian or Roman Catholic Churches, or indeed in no church at all. Ecumenical evening services with the Church of Scotland and Roman Catholic congregations in the village of Pitmedden attracted surprisingly large numbers – three hundred on one evening.

Outreach to the communities included the founding of a lunch club for the elderly, followed by a day care centre, as well as parent and toddler meetings, home groups, a Mothers Union branch, youth groups and a highly successful drama group for teenagers, *Dramatize*. Much time and effort was also put into the chaplaincy of nine schools and to developing an awareness of world needs through our companion parishes of Woodbury in the United States and Engcobo in Transkei, South Africa, and with a growing number of mission partners elsewhere in Africa and in Nepal, Palestine and Papua New Guinea.

Vocations to ordained ministry began to be discerned within both Saint Mary's and Saint James's and there are fifteen people currently serving as Episcopalian priests across the world who say that the call to ordination was formed or nurtured during their time in Ellon and Cruden Bay.

The Diocesan Synod of 1979, one of the last clergy only ones, was significant. During it Canon Ken Gordon proposed that an Eldership be formed in the Diocese of Aberdeen and Orkney. The Synod agreed and in Ellon the first Elders were commissioned by Bishop Fred Darwent in 1982 and in Cruden Bay a year later. They were ministers directly answerable to the bishop, with the role of working with the parish priest in pastoral care, compassion and love for the people. Along with this, very crucially indeed, went an encouragement to everyone in the congregations to use the gifts God had given them – everyone was thought of as having a ministry.

Bishop Bruce Cameron commissioned additional elders and at his request, with the encouragement of Canon Alice Mann from the Alban Institute in the United States, who faithfully stuck by us throughout the national *Mission 21* programme (and actually far beyond it), time was given to working out a Mission Statement. It was to set out the hopes and purpose of the congregations. A mission statement can be written very quickly, but if people are to feel part of it and be committed to it then it takes much longer. It took eight months just to get the fourteen words. They were (and still are) -

We seek to be churches filled with God's love, giving it away to others.

The strategies and tasks to fulfil this aim were also worked out, the most important being -

Joining in with whatever God is doing.

Jesus was very clear in the Gospels about Mission -
· Love God and one another
· Go and make all nations disciples
· Heal the sick
· Raise the dead

Saint Paul has very little to say about mission but much about faithfulness. In 2 Corinthians he says *When I am weak then I am strong* and he is making the point that if we do something because we think it's a good idea we may well be doing it in our own strength, which will run out eventually. Paul knew that he had just to join in with whatever God was doing and then he would be strong. This is an important element in the Ellon and Cruden Bay mission statement.

It encouraged us to realise that we did not have to be perfect or even to have special skills. What we had to do was be faithful and know and use all that God gives us. Terry Fullam, the Rector from Connecticut, told us on each of his visits that all the gifts needed were there amongst the people already, but that nobody had them all. For us it was to be a continuing, co-operative work of faith and love.

The Chronological Story of the 20th Century

1900 The United Presbyterian Church of Scotland and many of the Free Church of Scotland congregations unite to form the United Free Church of Scotland.

1901 Queen Victoria dies and is succeeded by her son, Edward VII.

1901 The Primus, Hugh Jermyn, resigns after fifteen years as Primus (he has been in ill-health for five years). He continues as Bishop of Brechin until his death in 1903.

The new Primus is James Kelly, who is sixty-nine and has been Bishop of Moray, Ross and Caithness since 1886. He had previously been Co-Adjutor Bishop of the diocese for a year and Bishop of Newfoundland in Canada from 1876-77, acting as co-adjutor bishop for the previous nine years). His link with Moray diocese dates back to his early days in Newfoundland where the diocesan ship, *Hawk*, had been provided by Bishop Eden. In Inverness he combined the role of bishop with that of Provost of Saint Andrew's Cathedral, which he resigns on becoming Primus.

1904 James Kelly resigns as Primus and three months later as Bishop of Moray, Ross and Caithness.

His successor as Primus is George Howard Wilkinson, who is seventy-one. He has been Bishop of St Andrews, Dunkeld and Dunblane since 1893, and was previously Bishop of Truro from

1883 to 1891. The new Primus was born in Durham and educated at the Grammar School there and at Brasenose College, Oxford. He was ordained in 1857 and served in parishes in London, Seaham Harbour and Bishop Auckland before becoming an immensely successful Rector of the fashionable Saint Peter's, Eaton Square, in London. He was nominated as Bishop of Truro by the Prime Minister, William Gladstone, and appointed by Queen Victoria. He oversaw the completion of Truro Cathedral and its consecration.

In 1891 Bishop Wilkinson resigned on suffering a breakdown in health and travelled to South Africa to recuperate, a journey which gave him an abiding interest in African mission. His health recovered within two years and he was elected Bishop of St Andrews, Dunkeld and Dunblane – the first (and so far only) English diocesan bishop to become a Scottish Bishop (although Brian Smith, Bishop of Edinburgh from 2002 to 2011, was elected while serving as Suffragan Bishop of Tonbridge). One of the Canons of St Ninian's Cathedral (a building which the new Bishop – as at Truro – saw to completion) described Bishop Wilkinson as having a "touch of holiness".

1905 The Provincial Synod agrees to the creation of a Consultative Council on Church Legislation, which gives laity a foothold in the Synod's decision making.

1907 The former Primus, James Butler Knill Kelly, dies in Inverness, aged seventy-two.

1907 The Primus, George Howard Wilkinson, collapses and dies soon after making a speech in the Representative Church Council Office in Edinburgh. He is seventy-four and has been Primus for three years.

1908 The new Primus is Walter John Forbes Robberds, aged forty-six and Bishop of Brechin since 1904. He is the first Scot to be elected Primus since William Skinner sixty-seven years earlier. He was born in Bengal, where his father was a chaplain with the Indian Ecclesiastical Establishment, and his education was at Banchory in Kincardineshire, Glenalmond, and Keble College, Oxford.

1910 Edward VII dies and is succeeded by his son, George V.

1910 The World Missionary Conference in Edinburgh paves the way for the formation of the World Council of Churches many years later.

1911 The Primus, Walter Robberds, presides over the Provincial Synod which approves *The Scottish Book of Common Prayer* (it is in essence the 1662 Prayer Book with the addition of the Scottish Communion Office). The number of Canons in the 1911 Code increases to fifty-three.

1914 *The Million Shilling Fund* enables the building of six new Episcopal churches in, or close to, Glasgow.

1916 The Primus, Walter Robberds, confirms Lady Elizabeth Bowes-Lyon at Saint John's, Forfar. Seven years later Lady Elizabeth marries the Duke of York, the future King George VI.

1921 The Westminster Parliament passes the Church of Scotland Act 1921, which confirms the independence of the Presbyterian Church of Scotland in spiritual matters. The Act is followed by the Church of Scotland (Property and Endowments) Act in 1925, which prepares the way for the union of the Church of Scotland and the United Free Church of Scotland in 1929.

1925 The Scottish Churches' Council is established in 1925 with representatives of the Episcopal Church, Church of Scotland, United Free Church, Congregational Church, Baptist Church and United Secession Church. The original intention is that it be an instrument in situations where concerted action is necessary. In 1948 and 1964 the aims are broadened. A residential and conference centre, Scottish Churches' House in Dunblane, opens in 1961. Declining use and increasing costs, however, causes the closure of the House in 2011.

1920s *The Home Mission Appeal* produces ten new Episcopal churches in the Dioceses of Glasgow, Edinburgh, Aberdeen, Brechin and St Andrews.

1929 The Primus, Walter Robberds, presides at the Provincial Synod which approves four years of work on revision of the Code of Canons and also gives approval to the complete *Scottish Prayer Book* (which is still in use). Among three new Canons is one recognising the Order of Deaconess, although making it clear that a Deaconess is not to be considered in Holy Orders.

1931 Conversations with the Old Catholics in Europe lead to inter-communion with the Old Catholic Churches in communion with the Metropolitan See of Utrecht, although formal approval waits until the next Provincial Synod meetings in 1951 and 1952.

1932-1970 The Episcopal Church is involved in four separate sets of discussions with the Church of Scotland (the first two also involved the Church of England and the Presbyterian Church of England) but no agreement on union is achieved. In 1970 a proposal that the Episcopal Church become a Synod within a (united) Church of Scotland is not taken further.

1934 The Primus, Walter Robberds, resigns through ill-health and moves to Tunbridge Wells for ten years of retirement, mostly as an invalid.

1935 The new Primus is the seventy-seven year old Arthur Maclean, Bishop of Moray, Ross and Caithness since 1904. The first Etonian to be a Scottish bishop, he studied at King's College, Cambridge, and was a lecturer in mathematics at both King's and Selwyn Colleges in Cambridge before being ordained in 1882 as a mission chaplain in the Diocese of Argyll and the Isles. In 1883 he was appointed priest of Saint Columba's, Portree, on the Isle of Skye, and became a fluent Gaelic speaker. Three years later he was appointed as Head of the Archbishop of Canterbury's Assyrian Mission, travelling throughout the Middle East, learning the languages and becoming an expert on Eastern Liturgy. He returned to Skye as Rector of Portree in 1891 and became Dean of Argyll and the Isles the following year. In 1897 he moved to Edinburgh diocese as Rector of Selkirk and was appointed Principal of Edinburgh Theological College in 1903. Within a year he was elected Bishop of Moray, Ross and Caithness. The 1929 Prayer Book owes much to his skill and scholarship. He was also the author of numerous books and articles, mostly concerned with the Eastern Churches or Liturgy

1936 George V dies and is succeeded by his son, Edward VIII, who abdicates eleven months later to be succeeded by his younger brother, George VI.

1937 The establishment of a World Council of Churches is agreed but its official inauguration, delayed by the Second World War, does not happen until 1948.

1942 The British Council of Churches is formed.

1943 The Primus, Arthur Maclean, resigns aged eighty-five and dies within three weeks. He became Primus after more than thirty years as a distinguished bishop and in his last years has to contend with deafness and the increasing frailties of age.
 His successor as Primus is Logie Danson, who is aged sixty-three and has been Bishop of Edinburgh since 1939. He was born in 1890 in Arbroath, where his father (later to be Dean of Aberdeen and Orkney) was Rector of Saint Mary's, Arbroath. He was educated at Aberdeen Grammar School, Glenalmond College and Aberdeen University. He trained for the ministry at Edinburgh Theological College and served a six year curacy at Saint Paul's Cathedral, Dundee. In 1911 he became a curate at Singapore Cathedral and in 1914 moved to Malaya as Chaplain at Negri Sembilan. Six years later he became Bishop of Labuan and Sarawak, aged thirty-seven. He returned to the United Kingdom in 1931 and became a Residentiary Canon of Carlisle Cathedral and Assistant Bishop in the Diocese of Carlisle. In 1938 he became Provost of Saint Mary's Cathedral, Edinburgh, and Assistant Bishop in Edinburgh Diocese. A year later he was elected as Bishop of Edinburgh.

1944 The former Primus, Walter John Forbes Robberds, dies in Tunbridge Wells, aged eighty-one.

1944 *The Home Mission Crusade* results in five new Episcopal churches in the dioceses of Glasgow and Edinburgh.

1944 The first women priests in the Anglican Communion are ordained in the Diocese of Hong Kong and Macao.

1946 Logie Danson resigns as Primus in May and as Bishop of Edinburgh in August, dying the following month aged sixty-six. His successor as Primus is John How, Bishop of Glasgow and Galloway since 1938. He was educated at Pocklington School and Saint John's College, Cambridge, and trained for the ministry at Ely Theological College. He was ordained in 1906 and was a distinguished priest in (successively) Cambridge, where he became the first Warden of the Oratory of the Good Shepherd, Diocesan Missioner in Manchester diocese, Rector of Liverpool and Vicar of Brighton. He might have been Bishop of Pretoria in South Africa or Archbishop of Brisbane in Australia but declined both appointments. He was fifty-six when elected Bishop of Glasgow and Galloway and sixty–two when he becomes Primus.

1951 Joseph Gray becomes Roman Catholic Archbishop of St Andrews and Edinburgh, aged forty-one.

1951 and 1952 The Provincial Synod meets in Edinburgh and makes a number of small amendments to the 1929 Code of Canons.

1952 George VI dies and is succeeded by his daughter, Elizabeth.

1952 John How resigns as Primus in March and as Bishop of Glasgow and Galloway in April. He becomes priest of two rural parishes in Somerset before finally retiring to Hove in 1955.

John How's successor as Primus is Thomas Hannay, aged fifty-five, Bishop of Argyll and the Isles since 1942. Born in Liverpool he was a student at Queen's College, Cambridge, at the time John How was a priest in the city. In his first year at Cambridge he heard a future Bishop of Zanzibar speak about the needs of Africa and resolved to work there as soon as possible. After a curacy in Yorkshire he went to Nyasaland under the auspices of the Universities Mission to Central Africa. He worked in Nyasaland (for two periods) and also in Kenya. He returned to England in 1926 and entered the novitiate of the Community of the Resurrection at Mirfield in

Yorkshire, making his profession as a monk in 1929. For seven years he was principal of the Community's theological college. He became known in Argyll as a retreat conductor and was elected Bishop of Argyll and the Isles in 1942.

1952 and 1954 The Scottish bishops say they have no objection to ordaining men in full-time work as non-stipendiary deacons and priests - but the "Regulations" needed to enable this take a further twenty-one years to appear.

1959 The Representative Church Council approves a suggestion by Provost Paddy Shannon of Saint Andrew's Cathedral, Aberdeen, that the Church should have an identical sign outside each church building. The following year the Lord Lyon grants Arms to the Church and a design is agreed which includes the shields of each of the seven dioceses. The design is still used today and makes each Episcopal Church easily recognisable.

1960 The Archbishop of Canterbury, Geoffrey Fisher, makes a private visit to the Vatican and meets with Pope John XXIII.

1960 The Primus, Thomas Hannay, presides over the Provincial Synod which decides that members of the laity should have a place in the Synod – replacing the Consultative Council on Church Legislation established in 1905. Two new Canons are added to the Code (concerning the confessional and the method of release from vows for a member of a religious community) and it is also agreed that the Provincial Synod should meet regularly and more frequently – previously it had only met (usually less than once a decade) when called by the bishops.

1961 The former Primus, John How, dies in Hove, Sussex, aged seventy-nine.

1962 Thomas Hannay, Bishop of Argyll and the Isles since 1942, retires after ten years as Primus. As a member of the Community of the Resurrection in Mirfield, Yorkshire, he returns to Mirfield in his retirement. The new Primus is Francis Hamilton Moncrieff, Bishop of Glasgow and Galloway since 1952. He is fifty-six. He was born in North Berwick and educated at Shrewsbury School and Saint John's College, Cambridge. He trained for the ministry at Cuddesdon College and served curacies in Cambridge and London. He became priest-in-charge of Saint Salvador's on the new housing estate of Stenhouse in Edinburgh and chaplain of Saughton Prison. He was appointed Diocesan Missioner for Edinburgh Diocese in 1951 and a year later was elected Bishop of Glasgow and Galloway, at the age of forty-six.

1963 and 1966 The Provincial Synod agrees a Canon which permits a cleric of any Trinitarian church to assist at a wedding, funeral or memorial service in the Episcopal Church. In 1966 this is extended to "a service or occasion of an ecumenical nature". Lay Episcopalians are also now permitted to assist the priest in the administration of Holy Communion.

1964 Leslie Drage is appointed the Episcopal Church's first Overseas Chaplain – the intention being that he spend half the year immersed in the life of a church overseas and the other half travelling through Scotland raising awareness of the worldwide Church. The post is discontinued in 1975 and the current Chaplain, David Bruno, is appointed Provincial Director of the Department of Mission in Cape Province, South Africa, and becomes Dean of Windhoek in Nambia, Southern Africa, in 1980.

1965 Michael Ramsey is the first post-Reformation Archbishop of Canterbury, to make an official visit to the Vatican and meets with Pope Paul VI.

1965 Ecumenical Communities of the Franciscan Hermits of the Transfiguration are established at Roslin (for men) and Loanhead (for women) with the joint encouragement of the Bishop of Edinburgh and Abbot of Nunraw.

1966 and 1970 The Grey Book Liturgies are published. They are revisions of the Communion Office of the 1929 Prayer Book.

1966 The Livingston Ecumenical Experiment begins – the Church of Scotland, the Congregational Church and the Episcopal Church (later joined by the Methodist Church) jointly minister to the new town of Livingston.

1967 Multi-Lateral Conversations on Unity begin. They involve the Church of Scotland, the Episcopal, Congregational, United Reform, Methodist and United Free Churches and continue for over thirty years. In 2008 the Episcopal, Methodist and United Reform Churches sign a Covenant Relationship with a commitment to working together more closely.

1968 The Church of Scotland opens all ministries and offices to women and men on an equal basis.

1970 The former Primus, Thomas Hannay, who returned to the Community of the Resurrection on his retirement in 1962, dies at Mirfield in Yorkshire. He is eighty-three and in the forty-second year of his profession as a monk.

1969 The Roman Catholic Archbishop of St Andrews and Edinburgh, Gordon Joseph Gray, is appointed a Cardinal, the first post-Reformation Cardinal to be resident in Scotland.

1970 The Provincial Synod appoints a Diocesan Boundaries Committee. Its interim recommendations (some years later) include the creation of a Diocese of Central Scotland by merging the Dioceses of Edinburgh, St Andrews and Dunblane; the abolition of the Diocese of Argyll and the Isles, with some congregations being added to Glasgow and others to Moray; and the linking of the Dioceses of Brechin and Dunkeld, with some of the northern congregations of Brechin being added to Aberdeen. The Episcopal Synod decides not to proceed with the recommendations (although Cove and Torry are transferred from Brechin Diocese to Aberdeen and Stirling from Edinburgh Diocese to St Andrews, Dunkeld and Dunblane).

1972 The increase in the frequency of meetings of the Provincial Synod, and its subsequent greater amount of legislation, requires a new edition of the Code of Canons.

One of the changes is recognition that the Primus, although not holding primacy, is able to act as other Primates do in his dealings with them. The first of a series of amendments of Canon IV "On the Election of Bishops" is made, a process which occupies the Provincial Synod and its successor (in 1982) the General Synod a surprising number of times.

Lay Readership is opened to both men and women but co-adjutor bishops (who ensured Episcopal succession in difficult days) and catechists (who ministered to scattered congregations in the absence of a priest) disappear from the Canons.

1972 The Methodist Church agrees to a proposal for a union with the Church of England but the initiative fails to gain a sufficient majority in the Church of England's General Synod. The Congregational Church and the Presbyterian Church of England, however, unite and become the United Reformed Church.

1973 The "Regulations" for non-stipendiary ministry in the Episcopal Church are produced and the first ordinations take place.

1974 A long campaign for women's ordination culminates in the irregular ordination of women priests in the United States. The American Church authorises women's priestly ministry two years later.

1974 Francis Moncrieff retires as Bishop of Glasgow and Galloway and Primus. He has been Bishop since 1952 and Primus since 1962. His successor is Richard Knyvet Wimbush. He is sixty-four and has been Bishop of Argyll and the Isles, since 1963. He was born in Yorkshire in 1909 where his father served for forty years as Rector of Terrington, as his father had done before him. He was educated at Haileybury, Oriel College, Oxford, and Cuddesdon College. On his ordination he immediately returned to Cuddesdon as College Chaplain, followed by a curacy and an incumbency in Yorkshire. He was appointed Principal of Edinburgh Theological College in 1948 and held the office for fifteen years until elected as Bishop of Argyll and the Isles.

1974 Thomas Winning becomes the Roman Catholic Archbishop of Glasgow.

1974 The Scottish Episcopal Church establishes a Policy Committee to look at, among other things, structures for the governance of the Church. It reports in 1978, recommending that a General Synod replace the Provincial Synod and Representative Church Council. The recommendation is accepted in 1980 and the first General Synod is held in 1982.

1977 The Experimental Liturgy - The Orange Book – is published, the first "modern" language Communion Office.

1977 Richard Wimbush retires as Bishop of Argyll and the Isles and Primus. He has been Bishop since 1963 and Primus since 1974. In his retirement he becomes priest-in-charge of two rural parishes in Humberside and assistant bishop in the Diocese of York.

The new Primus is Alastair Iain Macdonald Haggart, Bishop of Edinburgh since 1975. The new Primus comes from a Free Church of Scotland family and grew up in Hyndland, Glasgow. He became a member of Saint Silas' Church in Glasgow (which was not at that time part of the Scottish Episcopal Church) and was trained for the ministry at Edinburgh Theological College and Durham University. He was a curate at Saint Mary's Cathedral in Edinburgh, Saint Mary's, Hendon, in Middlesex, and Precentor of Saint Ninian's Cathedral, Perth, before becoming Rector of Saint Oswald's, Glasgow, and Synod Clerk of the Diocese. In 1959 he became Provost of Saint Paul's Cathedral, Dundee, and in 1971 Principal of Edinburgh Theological College. He was elected Bishop of Edinburgh four years later, at the age of sixty. He is committed to ecumenism and in the British Council of Churches is Chairman of the Division for Ecumenical Affairs.

1979 A Scottish referundum results in 51.6% support for the proposal for a Scottish Assembly. However, the number voting in favour falls just short of 40% of the total electorate - a condition stipulated in The Scotland Act 1978.

1979 The Provincial Synod removes subscription to the Thirty-Nine Articles of Religion (agreed at the Convocation of Laurencekirk in 1804) as mandatory for ordinands in Scotland.

1980 The Provincial Synod agrees that those who have been divorced may re-marry in church, subject to the approval of the diocesan bishop.

1981 The ordination of women as deacons is agreed by the clergy and laity of the Provincial Synod, but not in the House of Bishops, and therefore is vetoed.

1982 The General Synod replaces the Provincial Synod and the Representative Church Council. Similar changes take place in each diocese with the present day form of Diocesan Synod being created.

1982 The 1982 Liturgy – the Blue book – is published. It is a revision of the 1977 Experimental Liturgy. It remains in use (with the later addition of seasonal material) as the most up to date Scottish Liturgy.

1982 The Ministry of Elders begins in the Diocese of Aberdeen and Orkney. Elders are commissioned (for a three year renewable term) by the Bishop for a variety of ministries.

1982 John Paul II becomes the first Pope to visit Scotland.

1983 The Scottish Episcopal Renewal Fellowship is founded to encourage charismatic renewal in the Church.

1983 The requirement that clergy wear a cassock at meetings of the General Synod is removed.

1984 The former Primus, Francis Moncrieff, dies in Edinburgh, aged seventy-seven.

1985 and 1986 The General Synod agrees that women can be ordained as deacons and the first ordinations take place.

1985 Alastair Haggart retires as Primus and Bishop of Edinburgh. He has been Bishop since 1975 and Primus since 1977. The new Primus is Edward Luscombe. He is fifty-one and has been Bishop of Brechin since 1975. He was born in Devon and educated at Torquay Boys Grammar School. He began training for ordination at Kelham in Nottinghamshire but in 1942 was commissioned as an officer in the Hyderabad Regiment, serving in Burma and India, remaining in India until 1947. On his return to Britain he trained as a Chartered Accountant in Glasgow and was a prominent layman in the diocese. He resumed his training for ministry at Saint Boniface College, Warminster, Wiltshire, and was ordained to his home church of Saint Margaret, Newlands, Glasgow in 1963. He became Rector of Saint Barnabas, Paisley, before his appointment as Provost of Saint Paul's Cathedral, Dundee, in 1971. Four years later he was elected Bishop of Brechin.

1985 Cardinal Gray retires as Roman Catholic Archbishop of St Andrews and Edinburgh – he dies in 1993. He is succeeded as Archbishop by Keith O'Brien.

1988 The Society of Our Lady of the Isles, a women's community (partly Celtic, partly Franciscan and partly Carthusian in its Rule) is founded on the Island of Fetlar in Shetland.

1988 Women ordained priest in other parts of the Anglican Communion are given "sacramental hospitality" and permitted to minister during visits to Scotland

1990 Edward Luscombe retires as Bishop of Brechin and Primus. He has been Bishop since 1975 and Primus since 1985. Following his retirement he becomes a student at the University of Dundee, graduating as a Master of Philosophy in 1991 and Doctor of Philosophy in 1993. He lives in a village near Dundee and is the author of many books on the history and personalities of the Episcopal Church.

The new Primus is George Henderson, aged sixty-eight and Bishop of Argyll and the Isles since 1977. He was born in Oban and studied at Edinburgh Theological College and Durham University. On ordination he served as a curate for five years in Bridgeton in Glasgow before moving to the Diocese of Argyll and the Isles as Rector of Nether Lochaber and Kinlochleven. Two years later he was appointed Rector of Fort William. He served for twenty-seven years until his election as bishop. During this time he was also a Labour Councillor in Fort William, Provost of the Burgh and a member of Inverness-shire County Council as well as, successively, Canon, Synod Clerk and Dean of the Diocese of Argyll and the Isles.

1990 The British Council of Churches and Scottish Churches' Council are replaced by Churches Together in Britain and Ireland and Action of Churches Together in Scotland, known as ACTS. The Roman Catholic Church becomes a member of ACTS, causing the Baptist Union to withdraw its full participation.

1991 Deacons are included in the electoral body which elects each diocesan bishop.

1991 *"Million for Mission"* begins. It is a five year programme reaching into areas of deprivation. A million pounds, raised from the Church's assets, is used to fund the programme.

1992 *Forward in Faith* is founded in England to argue the "traditionalist" case against the ordination of women.

1992 George Henderson retires as Bishop of Argyll and the Isles and Primus. He has been Bishop since 1977 and Primus since 1990.

He is succeeded as Primus by Richard Holloway. He is fifty-six and has been Bishop of Edinburgh since 1986. The new Primus was born in Possilpark in Glasgow and grew up in Alexandria in the Vale of Leven. He was educated at Kelham, in Nottinghamshire, in the junior seminary run by the Society of the Sacred Mission, an Anglican religious order. After National Service in the Army he joined the Society's novitiate but later became a student at Edinburgh Theological College. He was ordained in the Diocese of Glasgow and served a curacy in the Gorbals before becoming Rector of Old Saint Paul's in Edinburgh. Twelve years later he was appointed Rector of the Church of the Advent in Boston, Massachusetts. After four years he returned to the United Kingdom as Vicar of Saint Mary Magdalene's, Oxford, and two years later was elected Bishop of Edinburgh.

1992 The Meissen Agreement encourages Eucharistic hospitality between the Evangelical Lutheran Church of Germany and the Church of England, but still does not - formally - extend to the other Anglican churches of Britain and Ireland.

1993 and 1994 The General Synod agrees that women can be ordained as priests, and the first ordinations in Scotland follow in December 1994.

Affirming Apostolic Order is founded as a traditionalist group in Scotland. It merges with *Forward in Faith* in 1997. (In 2013 the *Forward in Faith* website indicates that there are now no member congregations in Scotland but that there are three churches – in Aberdeen, Dundee and Fort William – "where the priest himself has declared that woman priests will not minister within his care of souls".

1994 The former Primus, Richard Wimbush, who retired in 1977, dies in York, aged eighty-five.

1994 Thomas Winning, the Roman Catholic Archbishop of Glasgow, becomes a Cardinal.

1994 Edinburgh Theological College is closed and replaced by the dispersed Theological Institute of the Scottish Episcopal Church.

1995 The College of Bishops discusses the abolition of the Dioceses of Argyll and the Isles and of Brechin. It is decided to leave the former in place but recommend that the northern part of Brechin diocese be added to Aberdeen and the southern to St Andrews. The proposal receives minimal support in the General Synod and is abandoned.

1995 A complete revision of the Code of Canons removes gender specific phrasing.

1995 *Mission 21* begins, with the Reverend (and soon to be one of the American Canons of Aberdeen) Alice Mann as consultant. The initial phase - *Making Your Church More*

Inviting - has an impact on many congregations across the country.

1996 The Scottish Episcopal Church signs the Porvoo Declaration, bringing it into full communion with the Nordic and Baltic Lutheran Churches, with inter-changeability of clergy.

1996 The former Primus, George Henderson, who retired in 1992, dies in Argyll, aged seventy-five.

1997 Further changes are made to Canon 4 (Canons are now numbered in Arabic rather than Roman numerals) on the election of bishops, enabling the electors to meet candidates.

1998 The former Primus, Alastair Haggart, dies in Edinburgh, aged eighty-two.

1997 A second Scottish referendum on the creation of a devolved legislature (the first was held in 1979) leads to the enactment of the Scotland Act 1998 and the re-creation of a Scottish Parliament a year later.

1999 The Reuilly Agreement between the British and Irish Anglican Churches and the French Lutheran and Reformed Churches, in effect, permits shared communion and looks toward a fuller unity.

Another Moment in the Century
Nuns come to Shetland

The Chapel of Christ the encompasser and All His Angels

On the Island of Fetlar it is difficult to avoid seeing the sea - sometimes calm and of the deepest blue, sometimes leaden grey in the haar and sometimes white in the fury of a gale. Few places on the island are out of sight or sound of the sea.

To reach Fetlar from almost anywhere is a considerable journey. Those who have their own boat might, in calm weather, think of anchoring in the Wick of Tresta, the bay off Aithness, but most visitors from afar will come to Shetland either by plane from Edinburgh, Glasgow, Aberdeen or Inverness or by the overnight ferry from Aberdeen to Lerwick, Shetland's capital.

It is a 12 hour voyage (more if the boat calls at Orkney en route) and, for those without a car, a bus can take northbound passengers on the 28 mile journey to Toft and a ferry to Ulsta on the Isle of Yell. Another bus ride, 20 miles across Yell to Gutcher, and another ferry journey. This time across the Bluemull Sound to Fetlar. All the ferries take cars as well as foot passengers and, in an effort to boost the number of visitors, there is currently no charge for people or cars travelling on the Fetlar boat.

Fetlar is the fourth largest of the Shetland Islands – six miles by five – and has around sixty people living there. The name comes from the Old Norse word for "prosperous" and reflects the fact that agricultural land is better than in the peat filled surrounding islands. The main settlement is Houbie, on the south side of the island. Fetlar's school and only shop are here. (Those coming to Fetlar should be aware that the shop is open for limited hours and also that there is no public transport and no fuel for cars available on the island).

A mile to the east of Houbie is Aithness and right at the tip of the Ness are the modern buildings of the Society of Our Lady of the Isles, looking over the Wick of Tresta and across the sea to the Out Skerries on the horizon. There is no overnight accommodation for guests but visitors are welcome in the Chapel. They are also welcome to make themselves tea and coffee in a nearby room. It is appreciated when the quiet and prayerful life of the Community is respected.

In 1984 Mother Mary Agnes (then Sister Agnes) came from the Franciscan convent at Posbury in Devon to begin a hermit life on the island, living in a tiny croft house with its byre turned into a chapel. Later she was joined by others and the Society of Our Lady of the Isles was founded in 1988. In Mother Mary Agnes' words - *"A Celtic lifestyle grew from Franciscan roots, and later, in its blossoming, began to bear fruit with a hint of Carthusianism....a recipe that blended all three, and more, resulted in something which was uniquely itself."*

The croft house and byre chapel are still there, the chapel dark and enfolding with pews and prayer desks created from the wood of the original cattle stalls. A light, and equally enfolding, new chapel of Christ the Encompasser and All His Angels, has been built as part of a new complex for the sisters. The numbers in the community have fluctuated over the years but it currently consists of two sisters in life vows; two oblates (known as companions, these two women live within the community and share in its work); other oblates living outwith Shetland and, finally, more than a 100 associates, members of the Caim, which is a Celtic word meaning "encompassment", the circle around the Community, sharings its values and ideals wherever they may live.

Daily life at Aithness is centred on God, the community coming together for the Mass and for some of the Prayer Offices, others being said in each of the separate hermitages. Tasks are shared among the community members – telephone calls received, letters and emails answered, the shopping done, the garden and buildings maintained. The lifestyle is so arranged as to provide for solitary and prayerful living within a community. The hour or so over coffee and cake after the Sunday Mass is welcomed both by community members and those who visit as a time of chat and relaxation.

The community was not the first religious house on the island. The earliest is thought to have been founded by Celtic monks who, in the 8th century, were massacred by Vikings – Gruting Bay on Fetlar is said to be where the Norsemen first came ashore in Britain. Nor is the Community of Our Lady of the

Isles the only convent today - Mother Mary Elizabeth, an Orthodox nun, lives elsewhere on the island.

On a hill behind the community's buildings at Aithness is a tangle of stones known as Hallaria-kirk. It was here that Mother Mary Agnes accepted her call from God to bring monastic life back to the islands. In her first book "*A Tide that Sings*" she wrote of this place -

"It had a very special feel, conducive to prayer, and had retained from who knows how many years ago the atmosphere of something sacred. A cold wind clutched at my cloak, and wrapping it more closely around me I perched on one of the scattered stones. Had a hermit perhaps lived here long ago? Why had it been dedicated to Saint Hilary, or perhaps it was Saint Hilarion? Had it been the church for this area of the island? Certainly it commanded a magnificent view. South over The Ness, east to Funzie and Everland, west over Houbie and to Tresta, and north to the Vord Hill; one could see the sea on almost every side. Why, though...? Why...? So many questions and why was I so magnetised to the Isles? Only the last question was I able to answer, and that now without a shadow of a doubt. I was magnetised because God was calling me to them."

Since the day that she entered the convent at Posbury at the age of twenty (and came to Fetlar twenty-one years later) Mother Mary Agnes has sought to live in obedience to God and to do everything for his glory. "*This*", she says, "*is what it is all about. It doesn't matter what we do, or how - whether it's sweeping the floor, or washing the dishes, answering letters or digging in the garden - so long as we do it for the glory of God.*"

The Society of Our Lady of the Isles is one of the Episcopal Church's hidden gems. Although difficult to find, the whole Church can value the women who live and pray there, providing a place of a-biding for Christ, a sacred place of worship and peace.

Mother Mary Agnes has written four books about the development of the community - "A Tide that Sings"; "The Song of the Lark"; "Island Song" and "For Love Alone". All were published in paperback by SPCK. "A Tide that Sings" and "Island Song" are out of print just now but second hand copies are sometimes available through www.amazon.co.uk

Chapter 9
The 21ˢᵗ century

In which women may be consecrated as Scottish bishops (although none have been). The Ordinariate is created and the sexuality debate begins in Scotland's churches.

The Chronological Story of the 21st Century (so far)

2000 Richard Holloway retires as Primus and Bishop of Edinburgh. He has been Bishop for fourteen years and Primus for eight. In his retirement he lives in Edinburgh and has chaired the Scottish Arts Council. He continues to write books as well as reviews and articles for several newspapers. From time to time he also presents radio and television programmes.

The new Primus is Bruce Cameron, who is fifty-nine and has been Bishop of Aberdeen and Orkney since 1992. He was born in Glasgow and came to the Episcopal Church through the Choir of Saint Margaret's, Newlands, becoming one of eighteen candidates for ordination from that congregation. He studied at Edinburgh Theological College and served two curacies – Helensburgh in Glasgow diocese and Davidson's Mains in Edinburgh. He became a chaplain at Saint Mary's Cathedral, Edinburgh, and youth officer for both the diocese and the Scottish Church. There followed a period as Rector of Saint Mary's, Dalmahoy, and chaplain to Anglican students at Heriot Watt University before joining the pioneering ecumenical team ministry in Livingston. His final ministry before being elected Bishop of Aberdeen and Orkney was at Saint John's, Perth.

2000 Further changes to Canon 4 removes the Office of Lay Elector (created in 1863) and transfers the role to each congregation's Lay Representative at the Diocesan Synod. Elections will now take place at a specially convened Diocesan Synod.

2001 Cardinal Thomas Winning dies in office as Roman Catholic Archbishop of Glasgow.

2003 A further change is made to Canon 4 as the General Synod agrees that women priests can be candidates for election as Bishops. (No woman has yet been elected and the name of only one woman has appeared on the published short-leets - the same person being nominated in two dioceses).

2003 The General Synod accepts two reports - *Journey of the Baptised*, which affirms that the basic context for mission is the local congregation, helped by the wider church, and *New Century, New Directions*, which presents a vision and strategy for ministry development.

2003 The Church of Scotland withdraws from the multi-lateral talks with other Scottish churches. The Episcopal, Methodist and United Reformed Churches continue the conversations and in 2008 enter a Covenant Relationship, with a committment to working together more closely.

2003 Keith O' Brien, Roman Catholic Archbishop of St Andrews and Edinburgh, is appointed a Cardinal.

2003 The Diocese of New Hampshire in the United States elects a bishop who is openly in a same gender relationship and the Diocese of New Westminster in Canada agrees a service of blessing for same sex relationships.

2004 Alison Elliot becomes Moderator of the General Assembly of the Church of Scotland for the year 2004-2005. She is the first lay person to hold the office since George Buchanan four hundred years earlier and the first woman to do so.

2004 An International Commission is established in the Anglican Communion to consider the decisions in New Hampshire and New Westminster and also where authority in the Church should reside. The Commission's report to the Primates, the Windsor Report, leads to a "Listening Process" in each Province and Diocese of the Anglican Communion, leading up to the Lambeth Conference of 2008. Moratoria are requested on the ordination of clergy in a same gender relationship, the blessing of same gender relationships and the incursion of bishops from any Province into another.

2005 The Scottish bishops say that homosexual orientation has never been a bar to ordination in Scotland (as the General Synod has not made a decision about it), but later - following meetings of the Primates of the Anglican Communion - the bishops accept the three moratoria. In 2013 they remain in place.

2006 Bruce Cameron retires as Primus and Bishop of Aberdeen and Orkney. He has been Bishop for fourteen years and Primus for six. In his retirement he lives in rural Perthshire, and has twice been Resident Scholar at Bruton Church, Williamsburg, Virginia, in the United States. He and his wife, Elaine, acted as interim Wardens of Scottish Churches House in Dunblane in the months before its closure.

He is succeeded as Primus by Idris Jones, who is sixty-two and has been Bishop of Glasgow since 1998. His election as Primus is unusual in that it is decided not by a vote of the bishops but by the drawing of lots. Idris Jones and Brian Smith, the Bishop of Edinburgh, each receive three votes in the Episcopal Synod and the deadlock cannot be broken in any other way. Of an, originally, Welsh family the new Primus was born in the English Midlands. He studied at the University of Wales at Lampeter and at Edinburgh Theological College and has worked in the Episcopal Church since 1980. During his time as Primus he becomes a patron of *Inclusive Church*, an organisation advocating a church which is open to all regardless of race, gender or sexuality.

2007 Sheilagh Kesting is the first woman minister to be appointed Moderator of the General Assembly of the Church of Scotland.

2009 Idris Jones retires as Primus and Bishop of Glasgow and Galloway. He has been a bishop since 1998 and Primus since 2006. In his retirement he lives in Ayrshire.

The new Primus is David Chillingworth. He is fifty-eight and has been Bishop of St Andrews, Dunkeld and Dunblane since 2005. He is the first Scottish bishop to be elected while serving in the Church of Ireland. He was born in Dublin and studied at Oriel College, Oxford and Ripon College, Cuddesdon. His entire ordained ministry was in Northern Ireland before his election as Bishop of St Andrews, Dunkeld and Dunblane. He is also the first Primus to write a blog on the internet.

2009 The sexuality debate is also taking place within the Church of Scotland. In May 2009 the General Assembly ratifies the appointment of the Reverend Scott Rennie (an openly gay man) as Minister of Queen's Cross Church, Aberdeen. The Assembly later agrees a moratorium on further such appointments, while homosexual ministers, ordained before 2009, may continue in office.

2010 Pope Benedict XVI visits Scotland, twenty-eight years after his predecessor, John Paul II, became the first Pope to do so. Later in the year the Pope announces the formation of an Ordinariate in which Anglicans (mostly those unhappy with developments concerning women's ministry and same gender marriage) can be welcomed into the Roman Catholic Church, whilst preserving parts of Anglicanism.

2011 The Ordinariate of Our Lady of Walsingham is created for the United Kingdom. Thus far two Scottish Episcopal priests have been re-ordained within it as Roman Catholic priests. Ordinariate Masses are currently celebrated in Fortrose, Aberdeen, Edinburgh and Stirling.

2011 The General Assembly of the Church of Scotland establishes a theological commission to report to the 2013 General Assembly on sexuality issues. Several ministers and congregations announce their departure from the Church of Scotland.

2011 The General Synod accepts the *Whole Church Mission and Ministry Policy* as a pattern to be followed over the next years. Each diocese with its bishop, takes a central place and is recognised as a source of new energy. The central structure of the Church is to act as an enabler and supporter and target its financial resources towards "missional endeavours".

2012 The General Synod rejects (by 112 votes to 6 with 13 abstentions) the request that the Scottish Episcopal Church sign the Anglican Covenant. The concept of a Covenant for the Anglican Communion arises from the Windsor Report and has been years in the planning. The Covenant's aim is to address the deep divisions across the thirty-eight Provinces of the Communion, triggered by the actions in the United States and

Canada. The Covenant seeks to replace the "bonds of affection", which traditionally holds the Anglican Communion together, with a more formal structure. The intention being that no Province makes a contentious decision without consulting the rest of the Communion. Having rejected the request to sign the Covenant, the Synod agrees to a motion asking the Archbishop of Canterbury, "to encourage the development of bonds of shared mission, respect and mutual support".

2012 In September The Scottish Government announces that the Parliament's legislation programme for 2012-2013 will include a Bill permitting same gender marriage in Scotland. Most main-line churches currently oppose it. The Episcopal Church in a statement in December 2011, coinciding with its response to the Government's draft Bill, said - *In submitting its response, the Scottish Episcopal Church has stated that its General Synod expresses the mind of the Church through its Canons. The Canon on Marriage currently states that marriage is a 'physical, spiritual and mystical union of one man and one woman created by their mutual consent of heart, mind and will thereto, and as a holy and lifelong estate instituted of God'.*

2012 The Church of England's House of Bishops removes the barrier on male priests in civil partnerships (provided they are celibate) from becoming bishops in England. Reaction to the English bishops' decision from parts of Africa and from the Primates of the Global South is unfavourable.

2013 In January the Succession to the Crown Bill, which, in effect, amends the 1701 and 1707 Act of Succession, is introduced by the Coalition Government at Westminster. Among the Bill's provisions is one which says " A person is not disqualified from succeeding to the Crown or from possessing it as a result of marrying a person of the Roman Catholic faith".

The Bill is clear that the monarch remains the Supreme Governor of the Church of England and that he or she cannot therefore be a Roman Catholic. The Archbishop of Canterbury, Dr Rowan Williams, just before he leaves office in December 2012 to become Master of Magdalene College, Cambridge, says that there also needs to be "a clear understanding that a future heir should be brought up in an Anglican environment".

2013 Saint John's Church in Aberdeen offers space for prayer in the church building to members of the neighbouring Mosque, which is too small for all its adherants to find a place inside. Those praying outside, in the cold of a northern winter, touch the heart of the Rector, Canon Isaac Poobalan, and leads to the offer, which is accepted as graciously as it was made.

2013 Three days before Pope Benedict XVI becomes the first Pope in 600 years to retire (rather than die in office) Cardinal Keith O'Brien, Roman Catholic Archbishop of St Andrews and Edinburgh, resigns as Archbishop amid allegations of improper conduct. He chooses not to be part of the conclave electing the new Pope. The conclave lasts just over twenty-four hours and elects the Cardinal Archbishop of Buenos Aires. He is the first Pope from the Americas, the first Jesuit to be elected, and the first Pope to take the name Francis. His installation is three days before that of Justin Welby as the 105th Archbishop of Canterbury. The two send each other messages of goodwill.

Chapter 10
What's Ahead?

In the wider world tensions continue, often focussed on the Middle East. Changes in the world economy and its banking systems are also taking place.

Who can yet say what may happen? There will be many significant times in the future, but as yet we do not know what they will bring.

However, in the Church in the years ahead there is likely to be much more on same gender relationships, tensions within the Anglican Communion, the attempt to redefine marriage in Scotland and, surely eventually, the election of a woman as a bishop in Scotland.

While, of course, changing trends in religious belief and the 2014 Scottish referendum on independence, whatever its result, will affect both Church and Nation.

However, as long as the Church, all the people of God, remains faithful to the teaching of Jesus, to love God and to reach out in care to all whose lives touch ours, then all shall be well!

Further Reading

These books are among those which provide a detailed history of the story of the Scottish Episcopal Church
(listed alphabetically by author)

Scottish Episcopal Clergy 1689-2000 – David Bertie (published by T & T Clark 2000)

Scotland: Church and Nation through Sixteen Centuries – Gordon Donaldson (published by the SCM press 1960)

The Episcopal Church in Scotland – Frederick Goldie (published by the St Andrews Press 1951 and 1976)

Episcopal Scotland in the 19th Century – Marion Lochhead (published by John Murray 1966)

First among Equals – Bishops who have held the Office of Primus of the Scottish Episcopal Church 1704 to 2012 – Edward Luscombe and Stuart Donald (published by Meadowside Publications Dundee 2012)

Bishops of Brechin 1689-2010 – Edward Luscombe (published privately 2010)

Steps to Freedom - Edward Luscombe (published by the General Synod 2004)

The Scottish Episcopal Church in the 20th Century – Edward Luscombe (published by the General Synod 1996)

Matthew Luscombe – Missionary Bishop in Europe of the Scottish Episcopal Church – Edward Luscombe (published by the General Synod 1992)

The Episcopal Church's Scottish Heritage – Martin Reith (published by the Company of the Servants of God 1984)

A Church for Scotland – the history of the Scottish Episcopal Church - Gerald Stranraer-Mull (published by the General Synod 2000, updated editions in 2006 and 2012)

Episcopalianism in 19th Century Scotland Rowan Strong (published Oxford University Press" 2002)

The Scottish Episcopal Church – a new history - Gavin White (published by the General Synod 1998)